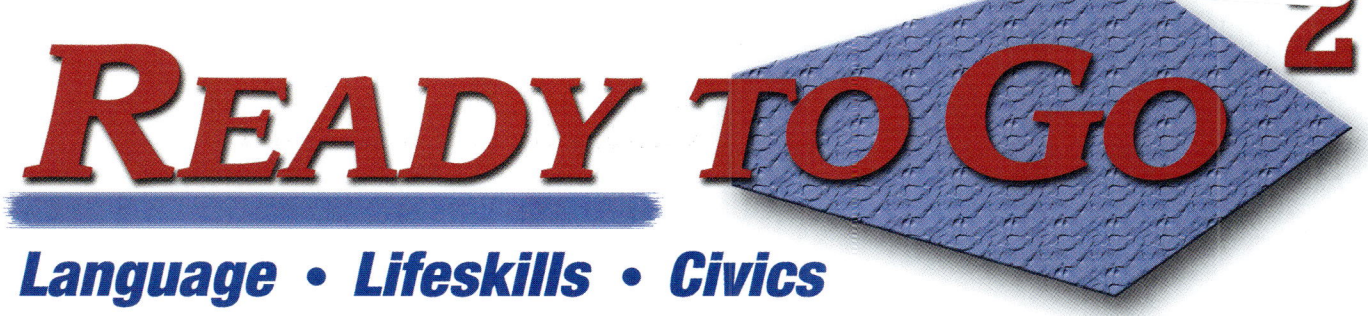

Ready to Go 2
Language • Lifeskills • Civics

Joan Saslow

Regional Consultant Board

Ann Belletire *Illinois*	**Sandra Bergman** *New York*	**Sherie Burnette** *Texas*	**Michael Feher** *Massachusetts*
Susan B. Kanter *Texas*	**Brigitte Marshall** *California*	**Monica Oliva** *Florida*	**Mary E. O'Neill** *Virginia*
	Grace Tanaka *California*	**Marcia L. Taylor** *Indiana*	

Tim Collins
Contributing Writer

Edwina Hoffman
Series Advisor

Longman

Ready to Go: Language, Lifeskills, Civics 2

Copyright © 2003 by Pearson Education, Inc.
All rights reserved.
No part of this publication may be reproduced, stored in a retrieval system, or transmitted in any form or by any means, electronic, mechanical, photocopying, recording, or otherwise, without the prior permission of the publisher.

Pearson Education, 10 Bank Street, White Plains, NY 10606

Vice president, instructional design: Allen Ascher
Senior acquisitions editor: Marian Wassner
Senior development editors: Jessica Miller-Smith and Marcia Schonzeit
Development editor: Peter Benson
Ready to Go development editor: Julie Rouse
Assistant editor: Patricia Lattanzio
Vice president, director of design and production: Rhea Banker
Executive managing editor: Linda Moser
Senior production editor: Christine Lauricella
Ready to Go production editor: Marc Oliver
Production supervisor: Liza Pleva
Ready to Go production manager: Ray Keating
Director of manufacturing: Patrice Fraccio
Manufacturing supervisor: Dave Dickey
Cover design: Ann France
Text design: Ann France
Text composition and art direction: Word and Image Design Studio Inc.
Ready to Go text composition: Lehigh Press
Illustrations: Craig Attebery, pp. 32, 33, 35, 55, 56, 80, 91; Crowleart Group, pp. 14, 15, 21, 33, 39, 50, 51, 52, 69, 91, 97, 99; Brian Hughes, pp. 18, 33, 42, 44, 45, 66, 92, 95, 100, 105; Paul McCusker, p. 23; Suzanne Mogensen, pp. 7, 10, 11, 22, 31, 33, 43, 46, 47, 58, 59, 67-71, 75, 84, 93, 94, 106, 107, 115, 118, 119; Dave McKay, p. 6; Dusan Petricic, pp. 47, 107; Stephen Quinlan, p. 11; NSV Productions, pp. 5, 19, 38, 43, 47, 74, 91, 95, 98, 102; Meryl Treatner, pp. 6, 7, 12, 34-36, 60, 72, 90, 91, 95, 96, 108, 114, 120; Word & Image Design, pp. 8, 11, 15, 16, 20, 21, 26-28, 39, 40, 43-45, 51, 56, 57, 59, 62-64, 69, 74, 75, 83, 86, 87, 88, 99, 103, 105, 110-112, 114, 122-124, 139-148; Anna Veltfort, pp. 9, 17, 21, 29, 41, 45, 53, 57, 65, 81, 89, 101, 113, 117, 125
Photography: Gilbert Duclos, pp. 2-5, 7-10, 13, 15, 19-21, 25-27, 31-33, 35, 37-39, 43-45, 49-51, 55-57, 59, 61, 62, 67-69, 71, 73, 74, 79, 80, 81, 83, 85-87, 92, 93, 97, 98, 103-105, 109, 111

Library of Congress Cataloging-in-Publication Data

Saslow, Joan M.
 Ready to go : language, lifeskills, civics / Joan Saslow, Tim Collins.
   p. cm.
   ISBN 0-13-177642-8 (v. 1) – ISBN 0-13-177644-4 (v. 2) – ISBN 0-13-177645-2 (v. 3) – – ISBN 0-13-177646-0 (v. 4)
   1. English language--Textbooks for foreign speakers. 2. Life skills--Problems, exercises, etc. 3. Civics--Problems, exercises, etc. I. Collins, Tim. II. Title.

PE1128 .S2755 2003
428.2'4--dc21   2002043418

LONGMAN ON THE WEB

Longman.com offers online resources for teachers and students. Access our Companion Websites, our online catalog, and our local offices around the world.

Longman English Success offers online courses to give learners flexible study options. Courses cover General English, Business English, and Exam Preparation.

Visit us at longman.com and englishsuccess.com.

---

1 2 3 4 5 6 7 8 9 10—WC—08 07 06 05 04 03

Contents

Scope and sequence	iv
Acknowledgments	viii
To the teacher	ix
About the author and series advisor	xii
Welcome to *Ready to Go*	2
Unit 1 Your life	6
Unit 2 The community	18
Unit 3 Technology	30
Unit 4 The consumer world	42
Unit 5 Time	54
Unit 6 Supplies and services	66
Unit 7 Relationships	78
Unit 8 Health and safety	90
Unit 9 Money	102
Unit 10 Your career	114
Vocabulary reference lists	
Alphabetical word list	129
Key expressions	132
Irregular verbs	135
U.S. postal abbreviations	136
Supplementary authentic documents	137

Scope and sequence

Unit	Lifeskills	Grammar	Social Language	Vocabulary	Civics/Culture Concepts
1 **Your life** page 6	• Make and receive telephone calls • Take and leave telephone messages • Read a weather map • Interpret information about weather conditions	• <u>Will</u> and <u>won't</u> for the future • Object pronouns <u>me</u>, <u>you</u>, <u>him</u>, <u>her</u>, <u>us</u> • <u>Would like to</u> + verb	How to • Answer the telephone at work • Take and leave a telephone message • Talk about the weather	• Weather-related terminology • Times of day • Meals	• Introduce co-workers or friends who don't know each other. (W)¹ • Understand and use telephone etiquette.
2 **The community** page 18	• Select housing by interpreting classified advertisements • Inquire about the neighborhood • Interpret lease and rental agreements • Fill out a rental information form	• Object pronouns <u>it</u> and <u>them</u> • Placement of two object pronouns in a sentence	How to • Ask about renting an apartment or house • Talk about a neighborhood • Ask about paying later	• Types of housing • Rooms • Places in the neighborhood • Household bills	• Signing a lease legally binds a renter to its terms. • Expect to pay a security deposit when signing a lease. • Rent may or may not include utilities. • Some landlords do not allow pets.
3 **Technology** page 30	• Report problems with vehicles and machines • Ask for an estimate • Schedule a repair • Interpret operating instructions and warnings • Fill out a repair order	• <u>It</u> and <u>them</u> with two-word verbs • The past continuous and the simple past tense • Review: object pronouns <u>it</u> and <u>them</u> • Review: the simple past tense	How to • Describe a mechanical problem • Leave a machine or vehicle for repair • Offer to call later	• Vehicles • Parts of cars and trucks • Products for cars	• It's OK to ask for an estimate before having a repair done.
4 **The consumer world** page 42	• Interpret advertisements • Compare prices • Request, offer, and fill out a rain check • Discuss a problem with a purchase • Apologize and offer to correct a mistake	• Comparisons with adjectives: comparatives • <u>One</u> / <u>ones</u> • Questions with <u>Which</u>	How to • Respond to a complaint • Clarify • Discuss an overcharge	• Personal care products • Medicines • Common drug-store items	• It's OK to ask for less expensive products. • Speak up about a possible overcharge. • Customers are entitled to return defective purchases. • Be aware of terms and conditions for sales.
5 **Time** page 54	• Use different types of transportation • Purchase and sell tickets • Interpret transportation schedules and fares • Explain lateness • Write an e-mail message	• <u>Should</u> • <u>Could</u>	How to • Buy a ticket • Ask about bus or train fares and schedules • Ask about lateness	• Transportation and commuting	• Be aware of fare-paying policies on public transportation. • Employees are expected to call if they are going to be late. • Understand schedules and plan ahead when using public transportation.

¹Welcome Unit

Math Concepts and Practical Math Skills	Critical Thinking Skills	Correlations to National Standards		
		SCANS Competencies	CASAS Life Skill Competencies[1]	EFF Content Standards[2]
• Understand and state telephone numbers • Interpret Fahrenheit temperatures on a weather map	• Reasoning (uses logic to draw conclusions from available information)	• Understands social systems • Interprets and communicates information • Demonstrates interpersonal skills	0.1.1, 0.1.2, 0.1.3, 0.1.4, 1.1.5, 2.1.7, 2.1.8, 2.3.3, 4.6.2, 7.5.7	A full range of EFF Content Standards is included in this unit. The following are emphasized: • Read with Understanding 1–5 • Convey Ideas in Writing 1–3 • Speak So Others Can Understand 1–3 • Listen Actively 1–4
• Understand spatial relationships • Compare rents • Calculate a security deposit based on rent • Apply concept of "maximum" in making rental decisions	• Decision-making (specifies constraints, evaluates and chooses the best alternative)	• Interprets and communicates information • Understands social systems • Serves clients and customers • Negotiates	0.1.1, 1.1.2, 1.1.3, 1.1.4, 0.2.1, 1.4.1, 1.4.2, 7.5.7	A full range of EFF Content Standards is included in this unit. The following are emphasized: • Read with Understanding 1–5 • Convey Ideas in Writing 1–3 • Listen Actively 1–4 • Take Responsibility for Learning 1, 3, 6 • Use Information and Communications Technology 1–3
• Understand concept of a cost estimate • Distinguish between a span of time and a point in time	• Problem-solving (recognizes a problem and implements a plan of action)	• Acquires and evaluates information • Interprets and communicates information • Serves clients / customers • Maintains and troubleshoots equipment	0.1.1, 0.1.2, 0.1.3, 0.1.4, 1.5.3, 1.9.5, 1.9.7, 7.5.7	A full range of EFF Content Standards is included in this unit. The following are emphasized: • Read with Understanding 1–5 • Convey Ideas in Writing 1–3 • Speak So Others Can Understand 1–3 • Listen Actively 1–4 • Take Responsibility for Learning 1, 3, 6 • Use Information and Communications Technology 1–3
• Understand and compare prices • Determine cost of items based on advertising and stated limitations • Understand U.S. units of measurement	• Problem-solving (recognizes that a problem exists, implements a plan of action to resolve it)	• Acquires and evaluates information • Negotiates • Understands systems	0.1.1, 0.1.2, 0.1.3, 0.1.4, 1.2.1, 1.2.2, 1.3.5, 1.6.3, 4.8.3, 4.8.4, 6.4.1, 7.2.3, 7.5.7	A full range of EFF Content Standards is included in this unit. The following are emphasized: • Read with Understanding 1–5 • Listen Actively 1–4 • Use Math to Solve Problems and Communicate 1, 3, 5 • Use Information and Communications Technology 1–3
• Calculate wait time • Based on intervals, calculate departure times • Select departure time in order to arrive before a certain point in time	• Decision-making (evaluates and chooses the best alternative)	• Serves customers • Understands systems • Acquires and evaluates information • Interprets and communicates information	0.1.1, 0.1.2, 0.1.3, 0.1.4, 2.1.7, 2.1.8, 2.2.2, 2.2.3, 2.2.4, 2.2.5, 2.3.1, 4.6.2, 6.6.6, 7.5.7	A full range of EFF Content Standards is included in this unit. The following are emphasized: • Read with Understanding 1–5 • Convey Ideas in Writing 1–3 • Speak So Others Can Understand 1–3 • Listen Actively 1–4 • Take Responsibility for Learning 1, 3, 6

[1] The corresponding CASAS Life Skill Competency List is available at www.longman.com/readytogo.
[2] A more extensive correlation to EFF Content Standards is available at www.longman.com/readytogo.

Unit	Lifeskills	Grammar	Social Language	Vocabulary	Civics/Culture Concepts
6 **Supplies and services** page 66	• Ask a favor of someone • Offer assistance with a job or chore • Politely decline an offer of assistance • Express thanks • Assess inventory and order supplies	• Agreeing with <u>too</u> and <u>either</u> • <u>A</u>, <u>an</u>, and <u>the</u> • The present continuous for the future • Review: the simple present tense and the present continuous	How to • Ask for and offer a favor • Accept or decline an offer • Express gratitude	• Bedroom and bathroom furniture, fixtures, and supplies	• It's OK to ask co-workers for help. • Offer to help co-workers. • It's important to express gratitude.
7 **Relationships** page 78	• Understand procedures and rules • Assess personal needs related to work schedules • Interpret and discuss personnel policies and job manuals	• <u>If</u> in statements about the future • <u>Had better</u> • <u>Would rather</u> • Review: imperatives	How to • Advise someone not to break the rules • Offer a choice • Ask for time to decide • Offer and accept advice	• Work, family, and community relationships • Relating to others	• Know where smoking is prohibited. • It's essential to know and follow an employer's policies. • Express concern for others' problems. • Employees are often entitled to family or parental leave and emergency childcare.
8 **Health and safety** page 90	• Give and understand warnings • Follow safety instructions • Write a note warning of a possible problem • Explain consequences of carelessness	• Responding with <u>I will</u> and <u>I won't</u> • <u>Might</u> • Review: <u>will</u> and <u>won't</u> for the future	How to • Warn someone about danger • Report a dangerous situation • Remind someone to do something	• Safety and danger	• Residents are often legally entitled to smoke detectors. • It's a duty to warn others and report dangerous situations. • Express gratitude for help.
9 **Money** page 102	• Open a bank account • Cash a check • Fill out deposit and withdrawal slips • Read a bank statement	• Comparisons with adjectives: superlatives • Questions of degree • Review: comparative forms of adjectives	How to • Ask for information in a bank • Ask how long something will take • Remember something you forgot to do	• Banking and check-cashing offices	• Expect to pay a fee when using another bank's ATM. • Customers are entitled to ask about terms of bank products and services.
10 **Your career** page 114	• Make a helpful suggestion regarding employment • Compare and contrast company policies and benefits • Understand paychecks and pay stubs • Complete a benefits enrollment form	• The present perfect with <u>already</u> and <u>yet</u>, <u>for</u> and <u>since</u> • <u>Be supposed to</u> and suggestions with <u>Why</u> • Review: past participles	How to • Ask about a benefits plan • Remind someone about an obligation • Express sympathy over loss of a job • Suggest solutions or alternatives	• Health insurance • Employer-paid benefits	• Be aware of company-paid entitlements. • Follow the rules set by your insurance company to ensure maximum healthcare coverage. • Express concern for another's misfortune and offer to help. • It is considered rude to ask about another's income.

Math Concepts and Practical Math Skills	Critical Thinking Skills	Correlations to National Standards		
		SCANS Competencies	CASAS Life Skill Competencies[1]	EFF Content Standards[2]
• Calculate difference between supplies in stock and supplies needed • Estimate supplies needed in a given situation	• Problem-solving (implements a plan of action to resolve a problem) • Reasoning (uses logic to draw conclusions from available information)	• Acquires and stores materials efficiently • Communicates information • Understands organizational systems	0.1.1, 0.1.2, 0.1.3, 0.1.4, 1.1.4, 1.1.7, 4.5.1, 4.7.2, 6.1.3, 7.5.7, 8.2.3	A full range of EFF Content Standards is included in this unit. The following are emphasized: • Read with Understanding 1–5 • Convey Ideas in Writing 1–3 • Use Math to Solve Problems and Communicate 1–3 • Cooperate with Others 1, 2, 4 • Take Responsibility for Learning 1, 3, 6 • Use Information and Communications Technology 1–3
• Determine amount of leave employees are eligible for	• Decision-making (specifies goals and constraints, evaluates and chooses the best alternative) • Reasoning (determines which conclusions are correct)	• Acquires and evaluates information • Interprets and communicates information • Understands organizational systems	0.1.1, 0.1.2, 0.1.3, 0.1.4, 0.2.4, 4.2.4, 4.5.1, 7.5.7, 8.2.3, 8.2.4	A full range of EFF Content Standards is included in this unit. The following are emphasized: • Read with Understanding 1–5 • Convey Ideas in Writing 1–3 • Speak So Others Can Understand 1–3 • Listen Actively 1–4 • Take Responsibility for Learning 1, 3, 6 • Use Information and Communications Technology 1–3
• Estimate how often activities are engaged in within a given period of time • Understand periodicity of time in maintaining fire safety equipment • Follow sequential directions	• Reasoning (determines which conclusions are correct when given facts and conclusions)	• Teaches others new skills • Acquires and evaluates information • Interprets and communicates information	0.1.1, 0.1.2, 0.1.3, 0.1.4, 1.4.8, 2.1.2, 3.4.2, 4.3.1, 4.3.3, 4.6.2, 7.3.1, 7.3.2, 7.5.7	A full range of EFF Content Standards is included in this unit. The following are emphasized: • Read with Understanding 1–5 • Convey Ideas in Writing 1–3 • Speak So Others Can Understand 1–3 • Listen Actively 1–4 • Use Information and Communications Technology 1–3
• Understand fees and interest rates • Calculate total deposit amount • Calculate checking account balance	• Reasoning (draws conclusions from available information)	• Understands systems • Acquires and evaluates information	0.1.1, 0.1.2, 0.1.3, 0.1.4, 0.2.1, 1.1.6, 1.3.1, 1.5.3, 1.8.3, 4.5.1, 4.8.3, 6.0.1, 6.0.2, 6.0.3, 6.0.4, 6.1.1, 6.1.2, 7.2.3, 7.5.7	A full range of EFF Content Standards is included in this unit. The following are emphasized: • Read with Understanding 1–5 • Listen Actively 1–4 • Use Math to Solve Problems and Communicate 1–3, 5
• Understand concepts of reimbursement and co-payment • Compare time requirements and benefits of vacation and sick day policies • Calculate net pay by subtracting deductions from gross pay • Correct math error in pay stub	• Decision-making (specifies goals and constraints, generates alternatives) • Problem-solving (devises a plan of action)	• Acquires and evaluates information • Understands organizational systems • Interprets and communicates information	0.1.1, 0.1.2, 0.1.3, 0.1.4, 0.2.4, 2.1.7, 2.1.8, 3.2.3, 3.2.4, 4.2.1, 7.5.7	A full range of EFF Content Standards is included in this unit. The following are emphasized: • Read with Understanding 1–5 • Convey Ideas in Writing 1–3 • Speak So Others Can Understand 1–3 • Listen Actively 1–4 • Take Responsibility for Learning 1, 3, 6 • Use Information and Communications Technology 1–3

[1] The corresponding CASAS Life Skill Competency List is available at **www.longman.com/readytogo**.
[2] A more extensive correlation to EFF Content Standards is available at **www.longman.com/readytogo**.

Acknowledgments

The author wishes to acknowledge with gratitude the following consultants and reviewers — partners in the development of *Ready to Go*.

Regional Consultant Board

The following people have participated on an ongoing basis in shaping the content and approach of *Ready to Go*:

Ann Belletire, Northern Illinois University–Business and Industry Services, Oak Brook, Illinois • **Sandra Bergman**, Instructional Facilitator, Alternative, Adult, and Continuing Education Program, New York City Board of Education • **Sherie Burnette**, Assistant Dean, Workforce Education, Brookhaven College of the Dallas County Community College District, Farmers Branch, Texas • **Michael Feher**, Boston Chinatown Neighborhood Center, Boston, Massachusetts • **Susan B. Kanter**, Instructional Supervisor, Continuing Education and Contract Training, Houston Community College-Southwest, Houston, Texas • **Brigitte Marshall**, Consultant, Albany, California • **Monica Oliva**, Educational Specialist, Miami-Dade County Public Schools, Miami, Florida • **Mary E. O'Neill**, Coordinator of Community Education, ESL, Northern Virginia Community College-Annandale Campus, Annandale, Virginia • **Grace Tanaka**, Professor of ESL, Santa Ana College School of Continuing Education; ESL Facilitator, Centennial Education Center, Santa Ana, California • **Marcia L. Taylor**, Workplace Instructor, Joblink, Ispat-Inland Inc., East Chicago, Indiana

Reviewers

The following people shared their perspectives and made suggestions either by reviewing manuscript or participating in editorial conferences with the author and editors:

Leslie Jo Adams, Santa Ana College–Centennial Education Center, Santa Ana, California • **Sandra Anderson**, El Monte-Rosemead Adult School, El Monte, California • **Marcy Berquist**, San Diego Community College District, San Diego, California • **Ruth Brigham**, A.C.C.E.S.S., Boston, Massachusetts • **Donna Burns**, Mt. San Antonio College, Walnut, California • **Eric Burton**, Downington Area School District, Downington, Pennsylvania • **Michael James Climo**, West Los Angeles College, Culver City, California • **Teresa Costa**, The English Center, Miami, Florida • **Robert Cote**, Miami-Dade County Public Schools, Miami, Florida • **Georgette Davis**, North Orange County Community College District, Orange County, California • **Janet Ennis**, Santa Ana College–Centennial Education Center, Santa Ana, California • **Peggy Fergus**, Northern Illinois University–Business and Industry Services, Oak Brook, Illinois • **Oliva Fernandez**, Hillsborough County Public Schools–Adult & Community Education, Tampa, Florida • **Elizabeth Fitzgerald**, Hialeah Adult & Community Center, Hialeah, Florida • **Marty Furch**, Palomar College, San Diego, California • **Eric Glicker**, North Orange County Community College District, Orange County, California • **Steve Gwynne**, San Diego Community College District, San Diego, California • **Victoria Hathaway**, DePaul University, Chicago, Illinois • **Jeffrey L. Janulis**, Richard J. Daley College, City Colleges of Chicago, Chicago, Illinois • **Mary Karamourtopoulos**, Northern Essex Community College, Haverhill, Massachusetts • **Shirley Kelly**, Brookhaven College of the Dallas County Community College District, Farmers Branch, Texas • **Marilou Kessler**, Jewish Vocational Service–Vocational English Program, Chicago, Illinois • **Henry Kim**, North Orange County Community College District, Orange County, California • **Dr. Maria H. Koonce**, Broward County Public Schools, Ft. Lauderdale, Florida • **John Kostovich**, South Texas Community College–Intensive English Program, McAllen, Texas • **Jacques LaCour**, Mt. Diablo Adult Education, Concord, California • **Beatrice Liebman**, Miami Sunset Adult Center, Miami, Florida • **Doris Lorden**, Wright College–Workforce Training Center, Chicago, Illinois • **Mike Lowman**, Coral Gables Adult Education Center, Coral Gables, Florida • **Lois Maharg**, Delaware Technical and Community College • **Vicki Moore**, El Monte-Rosemead Adult School, El Monte, California • **Deborah Nash**, School Board of Palm Beach County Schools, West Palm Beach, Florida • **Cindy Neubrech**, Mt. San Antonio College, Walnut, California • **Patricia Peabody**, Broward County Public Schools, Ft. Lauderdale, Florida • **Joe A. Perez**, Hillsborough County Public Schools, Tampa, Florida • **Diane Pinkley**, Teacher's College, Columbia University, New York, New York • **Kay Powell**, Santa Ana College–Centennial Education Center, Santa Ana, California • **Wendy Rader**, San Diego Community College District, San Diego, California • **Don Robison**, Jewish Vocational Service–Workplace Literacy, Chicago, Illinois • **Richard Sasso**, Triton College, River Grove, Illinois • **Mary Segovia**, El Monte-Rosemead Adult School, El Monte, California • **Laurie Shapero**, Miami-Dade Community College, Miami, Florida • **Sara Shapiro**, El Monte-Rosemead Adult School, El Monte, California • **Samanthia Spence**, Richland College, Dallas, Texas • **JoAnn Stehy**, North Orange County Community College District, Orange County, California • **Margaret Teske**, Mt. San Antonio College, Walnut, California • **Dung Tran**, North Orange County Community College District, Orange County, California • **Claire Valier**, School District of Palm Beach County, West Palm Beach, Florida • **Catherine M. Waterman**, Rancho Santiago Community College, Santa Ana, California • **James Wilson**, Mt. San Antonio College, Walnut, California

To the teacher

Ready to Go: Language, Lifeskills, Civics is a four-level, standards-based course in English as a second language. *Ready to Go* prepares adults for self-sufficiency in the three principal areas of their lives: the community, the home, and the workplace.

Communicative competence in English is of critical importance in achieving self-sufficiency. *Ready to Go* applies the best of current second language acquisition research to ensure immediate success, rapidly enabling learners to
- understand the spoken and written language of daily life.
- communicate orally and in writing.
- understand the culture and civic expectations of their new environment.
- master lifeskills necessary to survive and thrive in the American community and workplace.

To achieve these goals with efficiency and speed, *Ready to Go* weaves together three integrated strands: language, lifeskills, and civics*, tightly correlating the major state and federal standards with a complete language syllabus and relevant social language.

Course Length
Ready to Go is designed to be used in a period of 60 to 90 classroom hours. This period can be shortened or lengthened, based on the needs of the group or the program. The Teacher's Edition gives detailed instructions for tailoring *Ready to Go* to specific settings, circumstances, and student groups.

Components
Student's Book
The *Ready to Go* Student's Book is a complete four-skills text, integrating listening, speaking, reading, and writing, with lifeskills, math skills, civics concepts, and authentic practice understanding native speech and real-life documents. The book contains 10 units, each one followed by a concise review section. For lesson planning and compliance with curriculum guidelines, the Scope and Sequence chart (on pages iv-vii) clearly spells out the following elements for each unit:
- lifeskills
- grammar
- social language
- vocabulary
- civics/culture concepts
- math concepts and practical math skills
- critical thinking skills
- SCANS Competencies
- CASAS Life Skill Competencies
- EFF Content Standards

Further correlations of state and local standards to the *Ready to Go* course can be downloaded at no cost from the *Ready to Go* companion website at www.longman.com/readytogo.

In order to facilitate student-centered instruction, *Ready to Go* uses a variety of grouping strategies: pairs, groups, and whole class. In numerous activities, learners work with others to create a joint product. Those activities are labeled collaborative activities.

---

*In *Ready to Go*, the term "civics" refers to concepts that introduce learners to expected social behavior in this culture, an understanding of which is essential *before* students can participate fully or truly understand their rights and responsibilities as citizens. The term does not refer to citizenship education.

Two special features of *Ready to Go* are Do it yourself! and Authentic practice.

Because learners have an immediate need to use their new language outside the class, Do it yourself! provides a daily opportunity for students of diverse abilities to put new language into their own words. This affords them a chance to "try their wings" in the safe and supportive environment of the classroom.

Authentic practice activities create a "living language laboratory" within the classroom. Learners practice responding to authentic models of spoken and written English with the limited language they know. In this way, students build their confidence and skill in coping with the language of the real world.

Audiocassettes

Because listening comprehension is a fundamental survival and success skill for new speakers of English, *Ready to Go* includes a comprehensive listening strand in each unit of the Student's Book. In addition to listening comprehension activities, there are numerous other opportunities for learners to practice their listening skills. All exercises that appear on audiocassette are marked with a 🎧 symbol. A transcript of each listening comprehension activity is located on its corresponding Teacher's Edition page, for easy reference.

Teacher's Edition

An interleaved Teacher's Edition provides page-by-page teaching suggestions that add value to the Student's Book. In addition to general and day-by-day teaching suggestions, each teacher's page includes optional activities, language and culture notes that will help teachers demystify and explain new language to students, answers to all exercises, and the tapescript of each listening comprehension activity.

Workbook

In addition to the ample opportunities for reading and writing practice contained in the Student's Book, the *Ready to Go* Workbook contains further reading and writing exercises. The Workbook is valuable for homework or for in-class activities. An added feature is a test preparation activity for each unit, which readies learners for "bubbling in" and coping with the formats of standardized language tests.

Teacher's Resource Binder

A three-ring binder contains a wealth of valuable items to enable busy teachers to customize their instruction and make the preparation of supplementary teaching aids unnecessary. The Classroom Booster Pack provided with the Binder features pair-work cards, vocabulary flash cards, grammar self-checks, photo chat cards, and extension activities for daily use. Also included in the Binder are the following additional teacher support materials: Correlations of *Ready to Go* with state and federal standards, Student Progress Checklists, Pre- and Post-Tests and Achievement Tests, and Skills for Test Taking.

Placement Test

A simple-to-administer test places students accurately within the *Ready to Go* series.

Ready to Go Companion Website

The *Ready to Go* companion website (www.longman.com/readytogo) provides numerous additional resources for students and teachers. This no-cost, high-benefit feature includes opportunities for further practice of language and content from the *Ready to Go* Student's Book. For the teacher, there are optional strategies and materials that amplify the *Ready to Go* Teacher's Edition.

Student's Book unit contents
Each unit in the *Ready to Go* Student's Book uses an integrated five-step approach.

1. Vocabulary
   Essential vocabulary is presented in a picture dictionary format and followed by exercises.

2. Practical conversations
   Simple, memorable model conversations that are transferable to learners' own lives permit intensive practice of vocabulary and key social language. These are followed by lively pair-work activities.

3. Practical grammar
   Essential grammatical structure practice enables learners to manipulate the vocabulary and practical conversations to express ideas of their own.

4. Authentic practice 1
   A unique, real-world listening and speaking rehearsal, in which learners build their confidence and ability to interact in the world beyond the classroom.

5. Authentic practice 2
   A unique, real-world reading and writing rehearsal, in which learners build their confidence and skill to understand and use authentic documents that they will encounter in their own lives.

Review
Following each unit is a two-page review for learners to check their progress.

About the author and series advisor

Author

Joan Saslow

Joan Saslow has taught English as a second language and English as a foreign language to adults and young adults in the United States and Chile. She taught workplace English at the General Motors auto assembly plant in Tarrytown, NY; and Adult ESL at Westchester Community College and at Marymount College in New York. In addition, Ms. Saslow taught English and French at the Binational Centers of Valparaíso and Viña del Mar, Chile, and the Catholic University of Valparaíso.

Ms. Saslow is the series director of Longman's popular five-level adult series *True Colors, an EFL Course for Real Communication* and of *True Voices*, a five-level video course. She is the author of *English in Context: Reading Comprehension for Science and Technology*, a three-level series for English for special purposes. In addition, Ms. Saslow has been an editor of language teaching materials, a teacher trainer, and a frequent speaker at gatherings of ESL and EFL teachers for over thirty years.

Series advisor

Edwina Hoffman

Edwina Hoffman has taught English for speakers of other languages in South Florida and at the Miccosukee Tribe of Indians, and English as a foreign language in Venezuela. She provided teacher training in a seven-state area for federally funded multi-functional resource centers serving the southeastern part of the United States. Dr. Hoffman taught English composition at Florida International University and graduate ESOL methods at the University of Miami.

Dr. Hoffman is an instructional supervisor with the adult and vocational programs of Miami-Dade County Public Schools in Miami, Florida. She has acted as a consultant, reviewer, and author of adult ESOL materials for over twenty years. A graduate of Middlebury College, Dr. Hoffman's doctoral degree is from Florida International University.

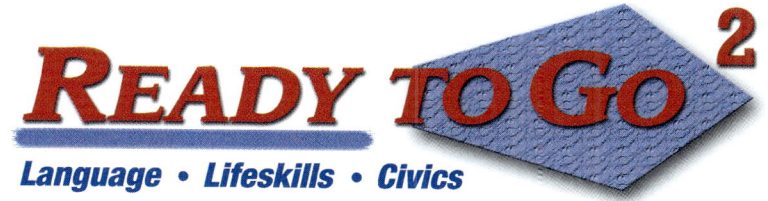

Welcome to *Ready to Go*

Practical conversations

Conversation 1 Greetings and introductions

 A. Listen and read.

1.
— Hi, David. How's it going?
— Great. What about you?
— Fine, thanks.

2.
— David, this is Teresa. Teresa, this is David.
— Nice to meet you, David.
— Nice to meet you too.

3.
— Where are you from?
— Me? I'm from Brazil. And you?
— I'm from Turkey.

4.
— And what do you do?
— I'm an electrician's assistant. I work in the parts department.

5.

🎧 **B.** Listen again and repeat.

▶ Do it yourself!

A. Introduce yourself to a classmate.

B. Now introduce two classmates to each other.

C. Make a chart. Write three classmates' names. Write their occupations. Write the countries they are from.

Name	Occupation	Country
Joseph	machinist	Korea
1.		
2.		
3.		

D. Tell the class about your classmates.

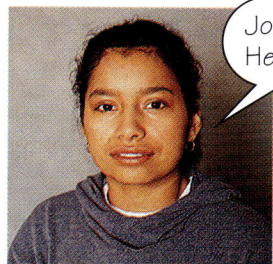

Joseph is a machinist. He's from Korea.

Welcome 3

Conversation 2 Clarification

A. Listen and read.

1.

2.

3.

4.

B. Listen again and repeat.

▸ Do it yourself!

Talk to three classmates. Clarify the spelling of their names.

Conversation 3 More clarification

A. Listen and read.

B. Listen again and repeat.

C. Pair work. Match each statement to the correct response. Then practice with a partner.

Statements

1. My number's 9085557806.
2. What's this called in English?
3. What does "breezy" mean?
4. My number is 908-555-7806.

Responses

a. It's a pickup truck.
b. Could you please speak louder?
c. Could you please speak slower?
d. It means windy.

UNIT 1

Your life

Vocabulary

Picture dictionary

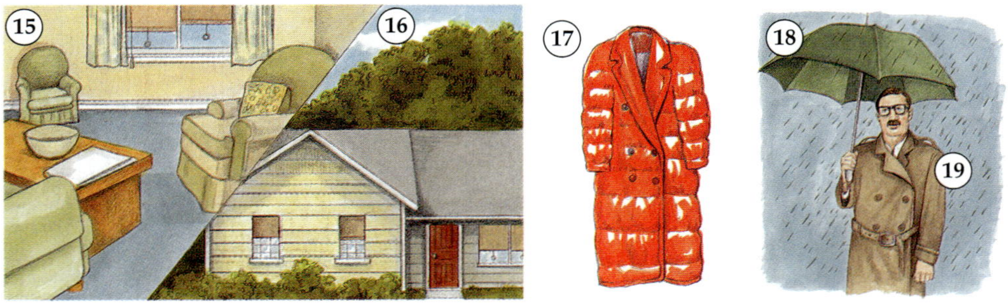

A. Listen.

Weather expressions	Times of day	Meals	Other words
① It's hot. ⑤ It's sunny.	⑨ in the morning	⑫ breakfast	⑮ inside
② It's cold. ⑥ It's cloudy.	⑩ in the afternoon	⑬ lunch	⑯ outside
③ It's warm. ⑦ It's raining.	⑪ at night	⑭ dinner	⑰ a coat
④ It's cool. ⑧ It's snowing.			⑱ an umbrella
			⑲ a raincoat

Objectives
- take telephone messages
- leave telephone messages
- talk about the weather
- read a weather map

Good and bad weather

⑳ good weather   terrific weather
   beautiful weather   great weather

㉑ bad weather   awful weather
   terrible weather   horrible weather

B. Listen again and repeat.

C. Listen to the conversations. Then listen again and match each picture with a conversation. Write the letter on the line.

Conversation 1 _____   a.    b.    c.

Conversation 2 _____

Conversation 3 _____

D. Complete each sentence. Write the word on the line.

1. It's 1:00 p.m. Let's have _____.
   _{lunch / breakfast}

2. It's _____ today. Let's eat outside.
   _{snowing / warm}

3. You don't need your _____ this morning. It's not cold outside.
   _{umbrella / coat}

4. The weather was beautiful yesterday. It was sunny and _____.
   _{raining / warm}

5. We eat _____ in the morning.
   _{breakfast / dinner}

▶ Do it yourself!

A. Personalization. Complete the chart about the weather and your clothes.

	Date	Weather	Clothes
Today	May 13	sunny and warm	a T-shirt
Today			
Yesterday			

Today it's sunny and warm. I'm wearing a T-shirt.

Yesterday it was cloudy and cool. I wore a warm jacket.

B. Discussion. Talk about the weather and what you wore.

Unit 1   7

Practical conversations

Model 1   Answer the phone at work.

A. Listen and read.

A: Copies Plus. Can I help you?
B: Yes, please. This is Jack Santos. I'm calling Jim Olcott. Is he in?
A: Yes, he is. Just a moment, please.... Jim? It's for you.

B. Listen again and repeat.

C. Pair work. Now use these companies and people. Or use your <u>own</u> company and people.

| Ace Cleaning Company | Victor Garcia |
| City Bus Service | Linda Lo |

A: _____. Can I help you?
B: Yes, please. This is _____. I'm calling _____. Is _____ in?
A: Yes, _____ is. Just a moment, please.... _____? It's for you.

Model 2   Offer to take a message. Leave a message.

A. Listen and read.

A: City Rentals.
B: Hello. Is Art Singer there?
A: No, I'm sorry. He's not in right now. Who's calling?
B: This is Ann Chang. When will he be back?
A: I'm not sure. Would you like to leave a message, Ms. Chang?
B: Yes. My number's 555-5021.

B. Listen again and repeat.

Message *Art:*
Please call Ann Chang.
555-5021

8   Unit 1

C. Pair work. Now use these companies and people. Or use your <u>own</u> company and people.

| Clearwater Plumbing | Steven Meng |
| Blake School Supplies | Tanya Golub |

A: _____
B: Hello. Is _____ there?
A: No, I'm sorry. _____ 's not in right now. Who's calling?
B: This is _____. When will _____ be back?
A: _____. Would you like to leave a message, _____?
B: Yes. My number's _____.

Model 3 Talk about the weather. Ask about messages.

A. Listen and read.

A: Oh, hi, Rita. What's it like outside?
B: Terrible. It's raining. By the way, are there any messages for me?
A: Yes. Andrea Lin called.

B. Listen again and repeat.

C. Pair work. Now use your <u>own</u> words.

A: Oh, hi, _____. What's it like outside?
B: _____. By the way, are there any messages for me?
A: Yes. _____ called.

▶ Do it yourself!

Pair work. Create a telephone conversation for the people in the picture.

Unit 1   9

Practical grammar

Will and won't for the future

Will Tom **be** back later?
Yes, he **will**.
Will he **be** back at 3:00?
No, he **won't**. He'll **be** back at 4:00.

When **will** they **be** in? — Later this afternoon.
Where **will** we **eat** lunch on Sunday? — Outside.
Who**'ll answer** the phones tomorrow morning? — Ms. Kim.

will + not = won't   I **won't call** Mr. Kapoor today. I'**ll call** tomorrow.

A. Where and when will you eat tomorrow? Write the places and the times. Then tell a partner what you'll do.

Tomorrow I'll eat breakfast at home at 7:00.

	Where?	What time?
Breakfast		
Lunch		
Dinner		

B. Write short answers about yourself. Use <u>Yes, I will</u> or <u>No, I won't</u>.

1. Will you eat lunch in a restaurant tomorrow? _____
2. Will you eat breakfast in English class on Monday? _____
3. Will you go to China this year? _____

Object pronouns <u>me</u>, <u>you</u>, <u>him</u>, <u>her</u>, <u>us</u>

They called **me** this morning.
Mr. Sorok left a message for **you**.
I'll see **him** tomorrow.
Please give **her** your umbrella.
They ate dinner with **us** yesterday.

Object pronouns
I	me
you	you
he	him
she	her
we	us

C. Complete each sentence with an object pronoun.

1. Do you want a job at Village Paints? Please talk to ____us____ on Monday.
   Marie and me

2. Give _____ an umbrella. It's raining outside.
   Mr. Loyola

10   Unit 1

3. This coffee is cold. Please bring _____ some hot coffee.

my daughter

4. Please give this message to _____. He's in the office.

your manager

5. Ms. Smith's not in? Can I leave _____ a message?

Ms. Smith

6. Please leave a message for _____. We'll call you back later.

Mr. Black and me

Would like to + verb

She'd like to
We'd like to   leave a message.
They'd like to

I + would like = I'd like

Would { you / he / they } like to eat lunch now? Yes, { we / he / they } would. / No, { we / he / they } wouldn't.

When would she like to go?   In the morning.
Where would they like to work?   At Village Paints.

D. Complete each sentence with a form of would like to and the verb.

1. I **'d like to leave** a message for my son.

leave

2. Please tell Patrick that we _____ to him in the afternoon.

talk

3. Our friends _____ inside. The weather is terrible.

eat

4. _____ you _____ in the morning or at night?

work

5. What kind of a job _____ she _____?

have

➤ Do it yourself!

A. Personalization. What would you like to do tomorrow? Make a list of three things.

B. Pair work. Now tell your partner what you'd like to do tomorrow.

Tomorrow I'd like to buy a new umbrella.

1. *buy a new umbrella*
2. _____
3. _____
4. _____

Authentic practice 1

With words you know, YOU can talk to this receptionist.

🎧 **A.** Listen and read.

Receptionist: Good morning. Paradise Travel. How may I direct your call?

YOU: *This is Jenny Lessing. I'd like to talk to Maggie Thomas.*

Receptionist: Just a minute, Ms. Lessing. I'll see if she's here.… I'm sorry, Ms. Lessing. She stepped away. Would you like me to tell her you called?

YOU: *Yes, please. My number's 525-7532.*

Receptionist: 525-7532. And is that L-E-S-S-I-N-G?

YOU: *Yes, it is.*

Receptionist: And how long will you be at that number?

YOU: *I'm not sure.*

Receptionist: Well, I'll tell her you called.

🎧 **B.** Listen to the receptionist. Read <u>your</u> part out loud.

🎧 **C.** Listen and read. Choose <u>your</u> response. Circle the letter.

1. "Health Care Center. How may I help you?"
   a. Yes, please.
   b. I'm calling Dr. Flynn.

2. "I'm sorry. She stepped away."
   a. When will she be back?
   b. Can I talk to her, please?

3. "How long will you be at that number?"
   a. For an hour.
   b. My number's 223-6511.

🎧 **D.** Listen. Choose <u>your</u> response. Circle the letter.

1. a. Thanks.
   b. Five minutes.

2. a. Just a moment. I'll check.
   b. Yes, please.

3. a. This is Peter Miller. Is Susan Preston there?
   b. This is Peter Miller. When will she be back?

Listening comprehension

A. Listen to the weather report. Then listen again and check ☑ the weather report you hear.

1. _____ today's weather in Miami
2. _____ tomorrow's weather in Miami
3. _____ yesterday's weather in Miami
4. _____ tomorrow's weather in Los Angeles

B. Critical thinking. Listen to the weather report again. Then answer the questions. Circle the letter.

1. What number did the caller press?   **a.** 2   **b.** 3
2. What will the weather be at night?   **a.** good   **b.** bad

C. In your own words. Answer the questions and then talk with a partner.

1. Where do you get information about the weather? _____

2. Why is it important to have information about the weather? _____

➤ Do it yourself!

A. Write your own response. Then read your conversation out loud with a partner.

Good afternoon. Mark Novak's office.
YOU _____

Oh, I'm sorry. He's not in the office today. Who's calling?
YOU _____

Would you care to leave a message?
YOU _____

B. Personalization. Talk about a telephone call you made.

Authentic practice 2

Reading

A. Look at the weather map. Then complete the sentence. Circle the letter.

The map tells about _____.   **a.** the future   **b.** the past

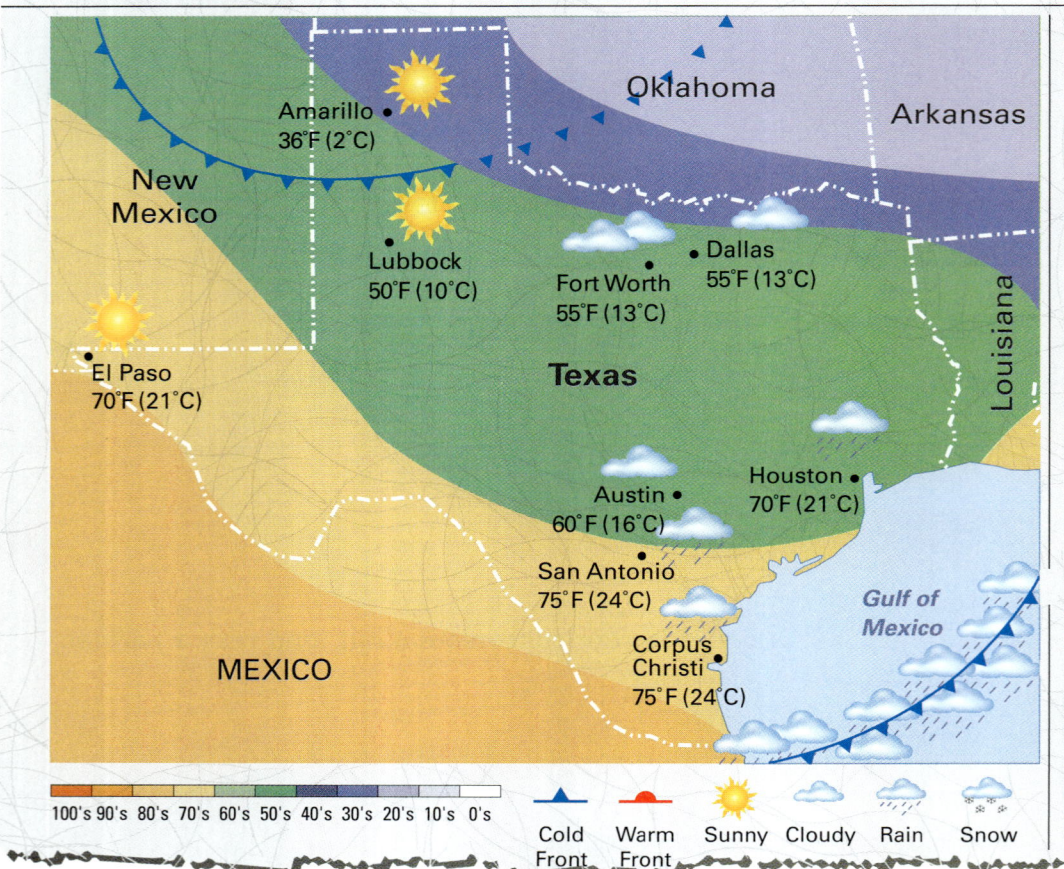

B. What will the weather be tomorrow? Write one or two words from the box for each city.

| cloudy   rainy   sunny   hot   cold   warm   cool |

1. Amarillo   _sunny and cold_
2. San Antonio _____
3. Lubbock   _____
4. Fort Worth _____
5. Houston   _____

14   Unit 1

C. Critical thinking. Look at the weather map in Exercise A. Choose advice for each person.

> You're in luck! The weather will be beautiful.

> You'll need a coat.

> You'll need an umbrella and a raincoat.

Gale

1. Jesse Gale lives in Amarillo. He has to work outside tomorrow morning. *You'll need a coat.*

Moreno

2. Luz Moreno lives in San Antonio. Her son Adam works in Houston. She wants to visit him tomorrow night. _____

The Riveras

3. The Riveras live in Austin. They have to go to El Paso tomorrow afternoon. _____

Writing

A. Listen to the conversation. Answer the questions.

1. Who called? _____
2. When did she call? _____

B. Listen to the conversation. Take a message for Mr. Ross.

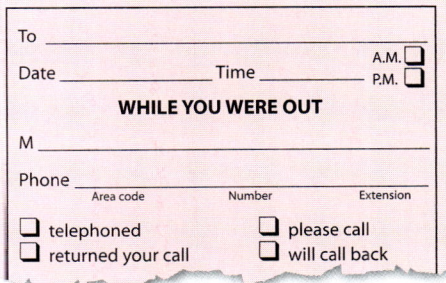

For extra practice, go to page 139.

▶ Do it yourself!   A plan-ahead project

Collaborative activity. Bring a weather map from the newspaper or the Internet to class. Talk about the weather. Prepare a weather report for the class.

> Tomorrow's weather will be cloudy and cool. The temperature will be 50 degrees.

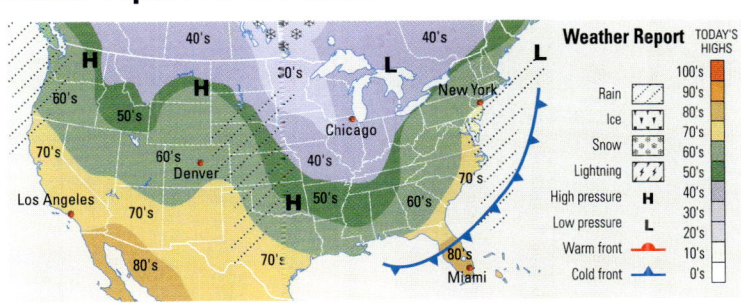

> # Review

A. Vocabulary. Complete each sentence. Write the words on the line.

1. The weather's _____ today. Take a raincoat and an umbrella.

terrible / terrific

2. When it's snowing, it's _____ outside.

warm / cold

3. When it's cold outside, it's a good idea to wear a warm _____.

umbrella / coat

B. Conversation. Choose <u>your</u> response. Circle the letter.

1. "Would you care to leave a message?"
   - a. Who's calling?
   - b. Yes. Please tell her I'll call back.

2. "Will you be at that number later this afternoon?"
   - a. I'm not sure.
   - b. 535-6622.

3. "I'm sorry. She won't be in today."
   - a. Will you be there later?
   - b. That's OK. I'll call back.

C. Grammar. Complete each sentence with an object pronoun.

1. They left ____us____ a message to call the factory.

my husband and me

2. Did they tell _____ who called?

you and your friend

3. Ron would like _____ to call back later.

Mrs. Rivas

D. Grammar. Complete each sentence with a form of <u>would like to</u> and the verb.

1. Please tell her that we _would like to talk_ to her tomorrow morning.

talk

2. _____ you _____ on Monday or Tuesday?

work

3. What time _____ she _____ lunch?

eat

E. Writing. Listen to the conversation. Take a message.

```
To _____
                                          A.M. ☐
Date _____ Time _____         P.M. ☐
            WHILE YOU WERE OUT
M _____
Phone _____
        Area code    Number      Extension
☐ telephoned              ☐ please call
☐ returned your call      ☐ will call back
```

16　Unit 1

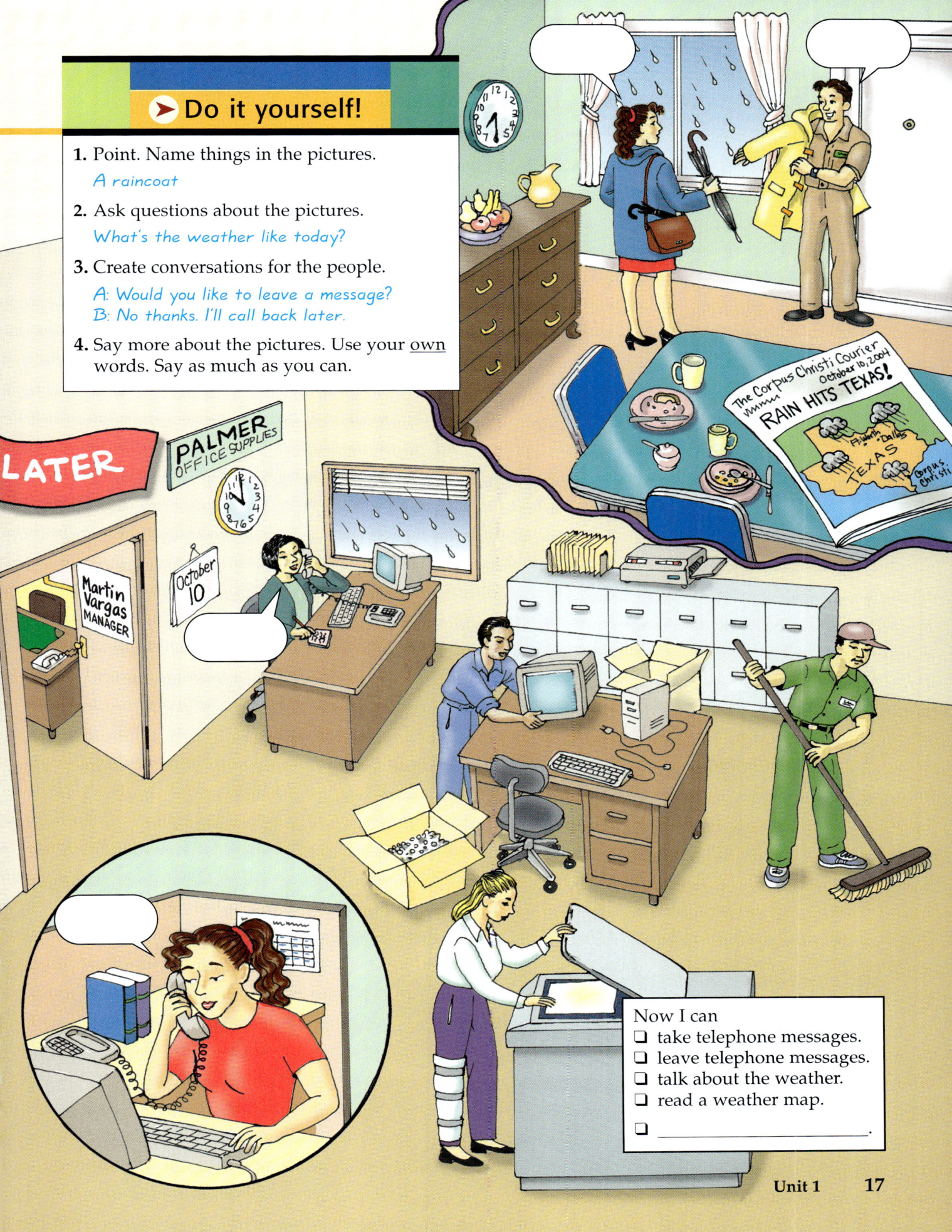

UNIT 2
The community

Vocabulary

Picture dictionary

Objectives
- rent a house or an apartment
- talk about rooms
- ask about the neighborhood

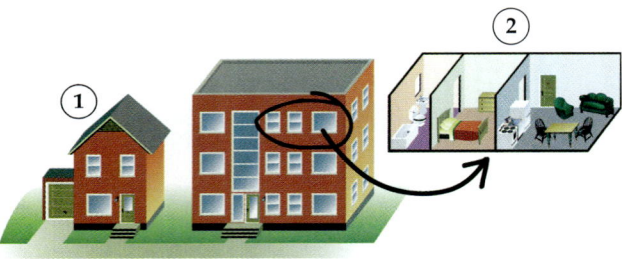
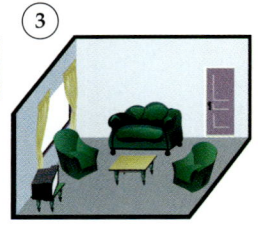
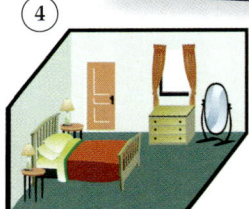
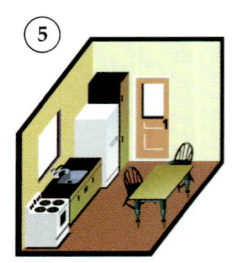
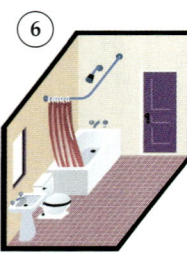
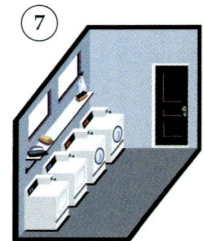

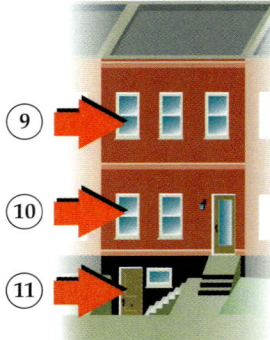

A. Listen.

Housing
1. a house
2. an apartment
3. a living room
4. a bedroom
5. a kitchen
6. a bathroom
7. a laundry room
8. an elevator
9. the second floor
10. the ground floor
11. the basement

The neighborhood
12. a bus stop
13. a subway station
14. a park
15. a convenience store

Other words
16. a gas bill
17. an electric bill

Expressions of location

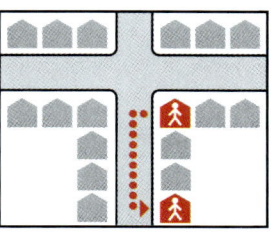
⑱ down the street

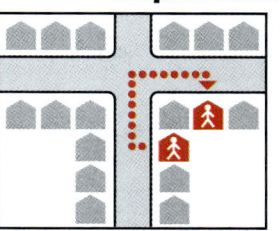
⑲ around the corner

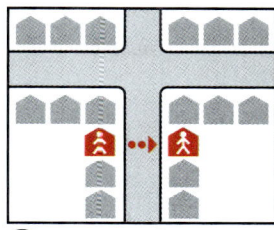
⑳ across the street

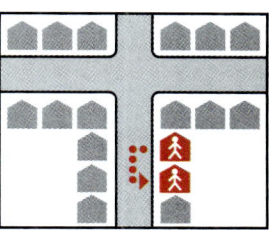
㉑ next door

B. Listen again and repeat.

C. Where are the people? Listen to the conversations. Then listen again and circle the letter.

Conversation 1   **a.** in the kitchen   **b.** in the bathroom

Conversation 2   **a.** in the bedroom   **b.** in the bathroom

Conversation 3   **a.** in the bedroom   **b.** in the laundry room

D. Complete each sentence. Write the words on the line.

1. The Kermians' new apartment has two _____.

                                                     ground floors / bedrooms

2. The apartment is _____, but that's OK because there's

                          on the ground floor / on the fourth floor

an elevator.

3. There's a _____ in the neighborhood.

              convenience store / bathroom

4. There's a park down the _____.

                              street / corner

5. There are a bus stop and a _____ around the _____.

                                    subway station / laundry room   corner / basement

➤ Do it yourself!

A. Personalization. Complete the chart about your neighborhood.

B. Pair work. Compare your neighborhoods.

Place	Location
a park	down the street
a convenience store	
a bus stop or subway station	
a school	
a _____	

In my neighborhood, there's a subway station around the corner.

Practical conversations

Model 1 Ask about renting an apartment or a house.

A. Listen and read.

A: I'm looking for an apartment in the neighborhood.
B: Well, there's a nice apartment on Beach Street.
A: How much is the rent?
B: $550 a month. Would you like to see it?
A: Yes. Can you show it to me today?

B. Listen again and repeat.

C. Pair work. Now use the <u>for rent</u> ads and your <u>own</u> words.

Rentals
FOR RENT
Center Street apartment
1 bedroom, 1 bathroom
$450 a month

FOR RENT
House, White Street
2 bedrooms
2 bathrooms
Rent: $700/month

Other times
today
tonight
tomorrow morning

A: I'm looking for _____ in the neighborhood.
B: Well, there's a nice _____ on _____.
A: How much is the rent?
B: $_____ a month. Would you like to see it?
A: Yes. Can you show it to me _____?

Model 2 Talk about the neighborhood.

A. Listen and read.

A: I have a few questions about the neighborhood.
B: Sure.
A: Is there a park nearby?
B: Yes, right around the corner.
A: And what about a bus stop or a subway station?
B: Yes, there's a bus stop across the street.

B. Listen again and repeat.

C. Pair work. Now use the map and your <u>own</u> words.

A: I have a few questions about the neighborhood.
B: _____.
A: Is there a _____ nearby?
B: Yes, right _____.
A: And what about a _____?
B: Yes, _____.

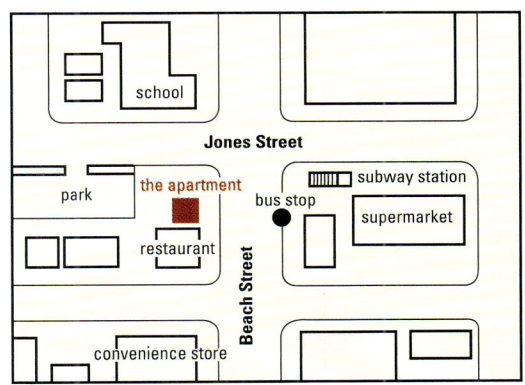

Model 3   Sign a lease.

A. Listen and read.

A: I'd like to rent the apartment.
B: OK. Here's the lease. Please read it carefully.
A: Thanks, I will. Is there anything else?
B: Yes. There's a security deposit. It's one month's rent—$550.
A: Can I give it to you tonight?
B: That's fine. No problem.

B. Listen again and repeat.

C. Pair work. Choose an apartment or a house from the ads on page 20. Talk about the lease and security deposit. Use your <u>own</u> words.

A: I'd like to rent the _____.
B: OK. Here's the lease. Please read it carefully.
A: _____. Is there anything else?
B: Yes. There's a security deposit. It's one month's rent—$_____.
A: Can I give it to you _____?
B: _____.

Rental Agreement

Term of lease: ___1 year___
Address: ___33 Beach Street___
Rent: ___$550 per month___   Security: ___$550___

▶ Do it yourself!

With two classmates, create a conversation for the people.

Ask about an apartment.
Talk about the neighborhood.

Unit 2   21

Practical grammar

Object pronouns *it* and *them*

A. **Complete each sentence with *it* or *them*.**

1. **A:** When did you rent your apartment?

   B: I rented _____ yesterday.
   _{the apartment}

2. **A:** Who paid the rent?

   B: Yoko paid _____.
   _{the rent}

3. **A:** Who fixed the elevator?

   B: I fixed _____.
   _{the elevator}

4. **A:** When can I paint the bathroom and kitchen?

   B: Please paint _____ today.
   _{the bathroom and kitchen}

5. **A:** I already cleaned the laundry room.

   B: You did? When did you clean _____?
   _{the laundry room}

6. **A:** Where are the keys?

   B: Right here. Do you need _____?
   _{the keys}

Placement of object pronouns

Give <u>this bill</u> **to her**. = Give <u>it</u> **to her**.

Please sign <u>this lease</u> **for me**. = Please sign <u>it</u> **for me**.

I'll give <u>these messages</u> **to her**. = I'll give <u>them</u> **to her**.

Pay <u>the rent</u> **for Mariana and me**. = Pay <u>it</u> **for us**.

22   Unit 2

B. Put the words in order. Write each sentence on the line.

1. They / for us / it / left / .   *They left it for us.*
2. Why / for her / it / are you cashing / ? _____
3. I'm going / it / for them / to pay / . _____
4. to us / them / Please / read / . _____
5. it / do / for me / Please / . _____

C. Write sentences with two object pronouns.

1. Please give the electric bill to Claire. *Please give it to her.*
2. Please read the ads to Mr. Pinto. _____
3. Please ask the Kermians for the security deposit. _____
4. Please clean the basement with Susan and me. _____

▶ Do it yourself!

A. Give some of these things to your classmates. Complete the chart.

Item	Classmate
keys	Jose
1.	
2.	
3.	
4. Your own idea: _____	

keys

a wallet

a checkbook

a driver's license

B. Discussion. Talk about what you did.

What did you do with your keys?

I gave them to Jose

Unit 2   23

Authentic practice 1

With words you know, YOU can talk to this apartment manager.

A. Listen and read.

Manager: Good morning. Can I help you?
YOU: Yes, please. I'm looking for an apartment. Are you the manager?
Manager: Yes. What size apartment are you interested in?
YOU: I need two bedrooms.
Manager: Let's see…. I have a couple of two-bedrooms available. One's right here in this building, and there's another one around the corner. Would you like to see them?
YOU: Well, how much is the rent?
Manager: The apartment in this building is $600. The other one is $700. But that includes utilities.
YOU: Excuse me? Utilities?
Manager: Gas and electric…. I see you have a dog.
YOU: Yes. Is that OK?
Manager: No problem in this building. But the one around the corner has a no-pet policy.
YOU: I'd like to see the apartment in this building. Can you show it to me today?

B. Listen to the manager. Read your part out loud.

C. Listen and read. Choose your response. Circle the letter.

1. "Is a one-bedroom OK?"
   a. Yes, that's fine.
   b. No. I have a dog.

2. "It's $900 a month, including utilities."
   a. What about gas and electric?
   b. That's too expensive for us.

3. "I have a couple of two-bedrooms available."
   a. Can you show it to me today?
   b. Can you show them to me today?

24   Unit 2

🎧 **D.** Listen. Choose your response. Circle the letter.

1. a. I need three bedrooms.   b. That's interesting.
2. a. Where is it?   b. Can I see it tonight?
3. a. No problem. I have two dogs.   b. That's OK.

Listening comprehension

🎧 **A.** Listen to the conversation. Then write yes or no.

1. The people are talking on the phone. _____
2. The people are talking about an apartment building. _____

🎧 **B.** Read the questions. Then listen again for the answers. Circle the letter.

1. When is the laundry room open?
   a. From Monday to Saturday.   b. Seven days a week.
2. When is the rent due?
   a. By the 10th of the month.   b. By the 25th of the month.
3. How much is the late fee?
   a. $10.   b. $25.

🎧 **C.** In your own words. Listen again. Answer the question and then talk with a partner.

What's Mr. Azizi's problem and how does he solve it? _____

▶ Do it yourself!

A. Write your own response. Then read your conversation out loud with a partner.

What size house are you interested in?
YOU _____

The security is one month's rent.
YOU _____

We have a no-pet policy. Is that OK?
YOU _____

B. Personalization. Talk about the rules in your apartment or house.

Authentic practice 2

Reading

A. Read the questions. Then read the ads and answer the questions.

1. How many apartments are for rent? _____
2. How many houses are for rent? _____

FOR RENT

① **HARRISON:** small 1 BR apartment. New eat-in kitchen, laundry rm in bldg, free parking. Nice neighborhood, near bus. $475 CALL (913) 555-6700 after 6:00 p.m.

② ***** LAKEVILLE *****
House 2BRS / 2BATHS.
Rent: $600 / month + sec.
Free parking. MAIN ST. RENTALS
(233) 555-0900 No pets

FOR RENT

③ **TWIN CITY**
Sm. 2- bedroom 1- bath apartment, next to supermarket and park. Free parking, $500 no lease, no deposit. No pets. (233) 555-7890

④ **MONTVILLE**
Apartment For Rent $400
1 bed 1 bth, 4th fl. elev. bldg.
Near bus stop and stores.
CALL AL AT (233) 555-4255

FOR RENT

⑤ **PARK VIEW**
$750, large house. 2 BR-1bath, across from park. New laundry rm in bsmnt. Pets OK. Call (913) 555-6522, ask for Diane

⑥ **CLAIRMONT** - Apartment 3BR / 2BTH, new fixtures. $600, util. included. No pets. Parking: $50 a month. Near subway. (913) 555-0827 or www.easyrental.com

B. Critical thinking. Read about the people. Which apartment or house is good for them? Write the number of the ad.

The Mees

1. Cynthia and Herman Mee want a one-bedroom apartment. They want to be near a bus stop. They can pay only $450 a month. _____

The Riveras

2. Hugo and Marta Rivera need an apartment or a house. They have two daughters, so they'd like two bedrooms and two bathrooms. They need parking for two cars. They can pay only $600 a month for rent and parking. _____

Farmer

3. Art Farmer and his son need a two-bedroom apartment. Mr. Farmer has a car, so he needs parking. _____

The Harrises

4. Wayne and Natasha Harris need a two-bedroom house or apartment. They have a dog. _____

Writing

Alvaro and Rosa Cordova need an apartment. They filled out a rental information form. Read their form and then fill out a rental form for yourself. Use your own information.

MAIN STREET RENTALS — No fee to renter. You need it. We find it.

Name: <u>Alvaro and Rosa Cordova</u>   Phone: <u>(773) 555-6487</u>
Current Address: <u>7521 Western Avenue, Chicago, IL 60626</u>
Housing needs: ☐ House   ☑ Apartment
bedrooms (number) <u>1</u>   bathrooms (number) <u>1</u>
rent (maximum) $ <u>400</u>
Desired location: <u>Chicago</u>   Neighborhood: <u>South Side</u>
Off-street parking needs: ☑ yes   ☐ no
Special needs: Check if important.
☐ pets   ☐ elevator   ☑ laundry room   ☐ bus/subway   ☐ parking

MAIN STREET RENTALS — No fee to renter. You need it. We find it.

Name: _____   Phone: _____
Current Address: _____
Housing needs: ☐ House   ☐ Apartment
bedrooms (number) ____   bathrooms (number) ____
rent (maximum) $ _____
Desired location: _____   Neighborhood: _____
Off-street parking needs: ☐ yes   ☐ no
Special needs: Check if important.
☐ pets   ☐ elevator   ☐ laundry room   ☐ bus/subway   ☐ parking

For extra practice, go to page 140.

▶ Do it yourself!   A plan-ahead project

"I like this apartment. It has two bedrooms."

A. Pair work. Bring apartment ads from the newspaper to class. Find one or two apartments that are good for you. Talk about the ads.

B. Collaborative activity. Talk about your own apartment or house with a partner. Then write an ad for it.

FOR RENT

_____
_____
_____
_____
_____

Unit 2   27

Review

A. Vocabulary. Complete each sentence. Write the words on the line.

1. My new apartment is on the ground floor. I won't need _____.
   _{an elevator / a convenience store}

2. The park is right around _____.
   _{the street / the corner}

3. The _____ is one month's rent—$745.
   _{security deposit / electric bill}

B. Conversation. Choose your response. Circle the letter.

1. "What size apartment are you interested in?"
   a. We need two bedrooms and one bathroom.   b. We need to be near the subway.

2. "Here's your new lease."
   a. Thanks. I'll read it carefully.   b. Can I pay it tomorrow?

3. "There's a convenience store right around the corner."
   a. Is it nearby?   b. That's good.

C. Grammar. Write sentences with two object pronouns.

1. Please give the lease to John. *Please give it to him.*
2. Please read the directions to Mrs. Tabor. _____
3. Please paint the bathroom for the Kermians. _____
4. Please clean the kitchen with Ellen and me. _____

D. Reading. Read the ads. Read about the people. Which apartment or house is good for them? Write the number of the ad.

1. Dennis and Fanny Tu need a two-bedroom house or apartment. They want two bathrooms. They can pay only $500 a month. ____

2. Ed Batista needs a two-bedroom house or apartment. He needs to be near a bus stop. He has a daughter, so he'd like to be near a school. ____

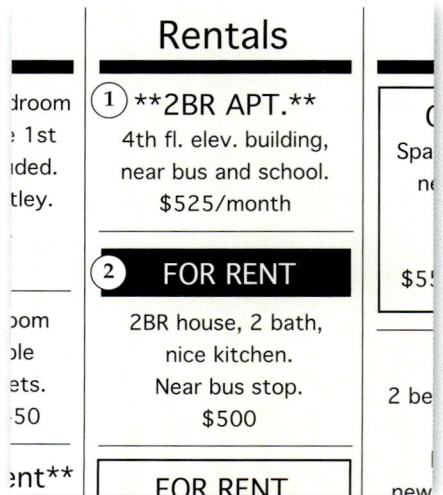

28   Unit 2

UNIT 3

Technology

▶ Vocabulary

Picture dictionary

Objectives
- report problems with vehicles or machines
- request service or repair
- ask for an estimate
- understand warnings

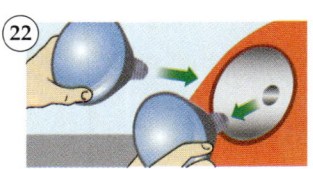

🎧 A. Listen.

Cars and trucks

1. a car
2. an SUV
3. a van
4. a truck
5. a tow truck
6. a pickup truck
7. a new car
8. a used car
9. a headlight
10. a hood
11. an engine
12. windshield wipers
13. a tire
14. a door
15. a window
16. a trunk
17. a brake pedal
18. a gas pedal

Products for cars

19. gas
20. oil

Actions

21. remove
22. replace
23. check

30   Unit 3

Two-word verbs

24. drop off 25. pick up 26. turn on 27. turn off 28. fill up

B. Listen again and repeat.

C. Listen to the conversations. Then listen again and match each picture with a conversation. Write the letter on the line.

Conversation 1 _____

Conversation 2 _____

Conversation 3 _____

a.  b.  c.

D. Complete each sentence. Write the words on the line.

1. I need gas. Can you please _____?
   drop it off / fill it up

2. It's raining. _____ the windshield wipers.
   Turn on / Turn off

3. Your car is ready. Please _____ today.
   drop it off / pick it up

4. I think the car needs oil. Could you please _____ it?
   check / remove

Do it yourself!

A. Personalization. What do you check, drop off, turn on, or replace? Complete the chart.

B. Pair work. Compare your chart with a partner's. Together, think of more items to add.

I turn on the coffee maker in the morning.

Check	1. *supplies*
	2. _____
Drop off	1. *mail at the post office*
	2. _____
Turn on	1. *the computer*
	2. _____
Replace	1. *old tires*
	2. _____

Unit 3   31

Practical conversations

Model 1 Describe a problem with a machine. Ask for an estimate.

A. Listen and read.

A: The door won't open.
B: No problem. Can you leave it here? You can pick it up at about five.
A: OK. Can you give me an estimate?
B: Sure. It'll be about $50.

B. Listen again and repeat.

Mechanical problems

won't open | won't go off
won't close | won't start
won't go on

C. Pair work. Describe a problem. Ask for an estimate. Use the words in the box or your <u>own</u> words.

A: The _____ won't _____.
B: _____. Can you leave it here? You can pick it up at about _____.
A: OK. Can you give me an estimate?
B: _____. It'll be about _____.

headlights	door	window
trunk	hood	engine

Model 2 Report a problem and schedule a repair.

A. Listen and read.

A: Auto Repair. Tony speaking.
B: Hello. I have a problem. My windshield wipers aren't working.
A: What kind of car is it?
B: A Monsoon SUV.
A: OK. Can you drop it off at about 10:00?
B: Yes. That's good for me.

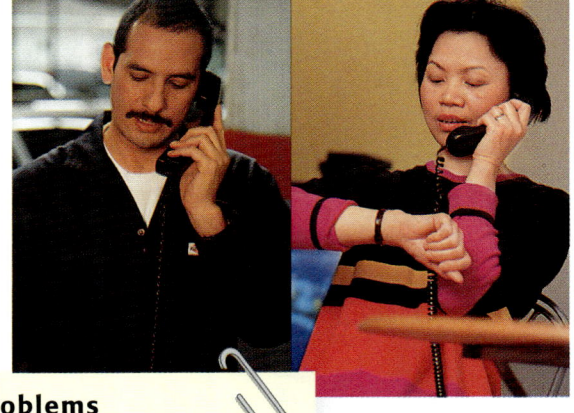

B. Listen again and repeat.

Problems

not working
making a funny sound

32   Unit 3

C. Pair work. Now use the pictures or your <u>own</u> words.

A: Auto Repair. _____ speaking.
B: _____. I have a problem. My _____.
A: What kind of car is it?
B: _____.
A: OK. Can you drop it off at about _____?
B: _____.

a horn   a radio

a turn signal

Model 3   Leave a car for a repair.

A. Listen and read.

A: I'm here to drop off my car.
B: What's the problem?
A: Well, I was driving to work, and my oil pressure warning light went on.
B: OK, I can check it for you.
A: Great! What time can I pick it up?
B: I'm not sure. I'll give you a call.

B. Listen again and repeat.

C. Pair work. Leave a car, van, or truck for repair. Use the picture and your <u>own</u> words.

A: I'm here to drop off my _____.
B: What's the problem?
A: Well, I was driving to _____, and my _____ warning light went on.
B: OK, I can check it for you.
A: _____! What time can I pick it up?
B: _____. I'll give you a call.

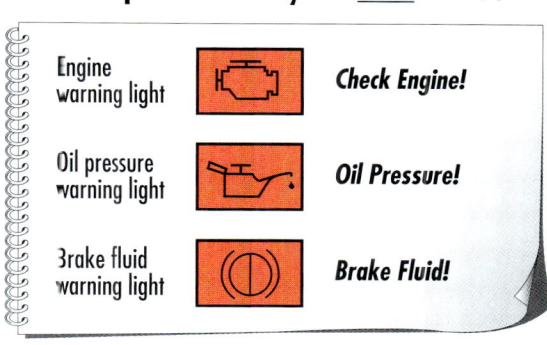

▶ Do it yourself!

A. Pair work. Create a conversation about a repair. Use the pictures or your <u>own</u> machine.

a TV

a VCR

B. Present your conversation to the class.

Practical grammar

It and them with two-word verbs

Review: One-word verbs

This door won't close. Can you **fix it**?

Two-word verbs

We can't fix your car today. Please **drop it off** tomorrow.

A. Review. Complete each sentence with it or them.

1. The windshield wipers aren't working. Please check _____.
2. The window won't open. Can she replace _____?
3. I can't change these tires. Will you change _____ for me?
4. The headlights won't go on. Is he going to fix _____?

B. Put the underlined words in order. Write each sentence on the line.

1. The windshield wipers aren't working.   can't / I / on / them / turn /.
   I can't turn them on.

2. My car needs new tires.   it / Can / off / drop / I / later /?
   _____

3. I have to turn on the headlights.   button / on / turns / them / Which /?
   _____

4. I'd like to pick up my car today.   up / can / I / pick / it / What time /?
   _____

5. I need gas.   Please / it / fill / up /.
   _____

The past continuous

I **wasn't driving** a new car.
Was she **driving** an SUV? Yes, she **was**.
Who **was driving** the car? I **was**.
What kind of car **were** they **driving**? A Monsoon van.

C. Complete the paragraph with the past continuous. Write the words on the line.

Ann Del Rio's SUV _____ a funny sound, and she wanted a mechanic to check
                    1. make

her car. But Marcus _____ the oil in a customer's used van. Antonio _____
                     2. change   3. replace

the headlights. Josef _____ the engine, and Donna _____ the old tires.
                      4. fix   5. remove

Even Al, the manager, was busy. He _____ on the phone.
                                    6. talk

The past continuous and the simple past tense

> The past continuous shows an action that continued in the past.
> The simple past tense shows an action that happened once and then stopped.
>   past continuous   simple past tense
> I **was eating** lunch when she **called**.

D. Choose the past continuous or the simple past tense. Write the verb on the line.

Yesterday I _____ the car ads in the newspaper when my sister
            1. read / was reading

_____. She _____ me what I _____, and I
2. called / was calling 3. asked / was asking   4. did / was doing

_____ her. So after work, she _____ with me to a used car lot.
5. told / was telling   6. went / was going

The manager of the lot _____ us a nice car, and I _____ it!
                       7. showed / was showing   8. bought / was buying

▶ Do it yourself!

A. Pair work. Ask your partner questions beginning with "What were you doing?" Use these times.

This morning   Yesterday

B. Discussion. Tell the class what your partner was doing.

Authentic practice 1

With words you know, YOU can talk to this driver.

A. Listen and read.

Driver: Bad news. Van 13 won't start.

YOU: Van 13? Really? It was working this morning.

Driver: I know. It started fine. But when I was leaving the parking lot, it just stopped. Right in the middle of the exit.

YOU: Excuse me? Where?

Driver: In the exit. I called maintenance. They're working on it now. But I need to pick up 18 kids. I'm already late.

YOU: No problem. You can have van 4. Emil dropped it off at noon.

Driver: Great. Where can I pick it up?

YOU: Outside. Next to the door. Here are the keys.

Driver: Thanks. I owe you one.

B. Listen to the driver. Read your part out loud.

C. Listen and read. Choose your response. Circle the letter.

1. "Bad news."
   - a. What's the problem?
   - b. Can I give them to you tomorrow?

2. "Where can I drop it off?"
   - a. I'll give you an estimate.
   - b. At Tony's Auto Repair.

3. "Thanks. I owe you one."
   - a. Please give me two.
   - b. You're welcome.

D. Listen. Choose your response. Circle the letter.

1. a. Oh, no.   b. Turn it off.
2. a. What time is Marie going to drop it off?   b. That's great. Thanks.
3. a. I don't know. It was working yesterday.   b. No problem.

Listening comprehension

A. Listen to the conversation. Then listen again and answer the questions. Circle the letter.

1. Where are the people?
   - a. At home.
   - b. In a repair shop.
2. What's the problem?
   - a. The VCR doesn't work.
   - b. The repair is too expensive.

B. Listen to the conversation again. Check ☑ yes, no, or I don't know.

	yes	no	I don't know
1. She wants to buy a new VCR.	❏	❏	❏
2. The VCR was working this morning.	❏	❏	❏
3. He can fix the VCR.	❏	❏	❏
4. She has to drop off the VCR tomorrow.	❏	❏	❏
5. He gave her an estimate.	❏	❏	❏
6. She'll call him tomorrow.	❏	❏	❏

C. In your own words. Listen again. Answer the questions and then talk with a partner.

1. What's the problem? _____
2. What is the customer going to do? _____

➤ Do it yourself!

A. Write your own response. Then read your conversation out loud with a partner.

- What's the problem with the TV?
  - YOU _____
- Well, I can take a look at it this afternoon. OK?
  - YOU _____
- Can you give me a number where I can call you with an estimate?
  - YOU _____

B. Personalization. Talk about a problem with your own vehicle or machine.

Authentic practice 2

Reading

A. Look at the owner's manual. Read the instructions.

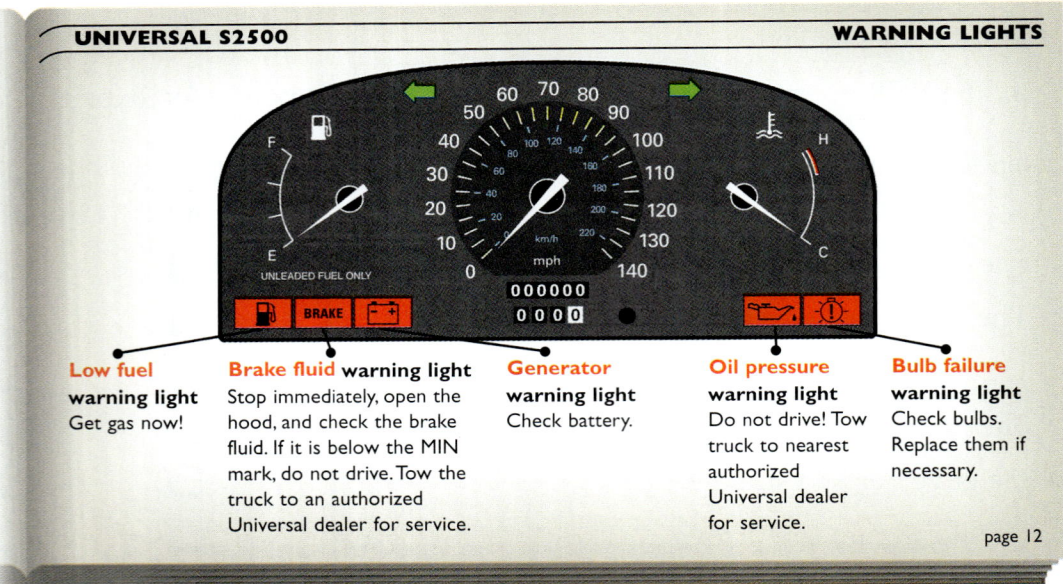

B. Critical thinking. Look at the three warning lights. These people were driving their Universal pickup trucks when the warning lights went on. What do they have to do? Circle the letter.

Lim

1. Ms. Lim has to _____.
   a. fill the car with gas
   b. check the brake fluid

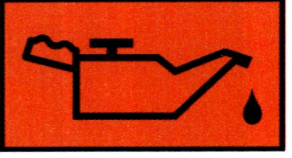 

Montoya

2. Mr. Montoya has to _____.
   a. stop driving and tow his truck to the dealer
   b. replace the bulb

Baraf

3. Ms. Baraf has to _____.
   a. replace the bulb
   b. stop driving and check the battery

38   Unit 3

Writing

A. Read Ms. Lim's repair order at the Universal Truck dealership. Answer the questions.

UNIVERSAL CARS AND TRUCKS

Repair/Service Work Order

NAME	DATE
Connie Lim	April 2, 2002

ADDRESS
3601 North Highway
San Antonio TX 78202

PHONE NUMBER
(210) 555-3766

MODEL AND YEAR	LICENSE PLATE NUMBER
330 Super Pickup 1999	G45 OKJ

Describe problem
I was driving to work and the brake fluid light came on.

Estimate	Drop-off time	Pick-up time
$85 00	8:20 a.m.	4:30 p.m. (will call)

1. What is the model name of Ms. Lim's truck? _____
2. When will her truck be ready? _____

B. Collaborative activity. Create a conversation with a partner. Then fill out the repair order together.

Partner A: You have a 2001 Monsoon SUV, license plate CO 3241. You were driving home from work when the oil pressure warning light came on.

Partner B: You work at the Monsoon repair shop.

Monsoon Cars and Trucks
7242

REPAIR/SERVICE WORK ORDER

DESCRIPTION OF PROBLEM

ESTIMATE

TOTAL

NAME | DATE
ADDRESS
PHONE NUMBER | LICENSE PLATE NUMBER
MODEL AND YEAR
DROP-OFF TIME
PICK-UP TIME

For extra practice, go to page 141.

▶ Do it yourself! A plan-ahead project

Discussion. Bring in a manual for a car or for a machine or use the one here. Talk about the warnings.

"Do not use any appliance with a damaged cord or plug."

Do not spill liquids on the machine.

Unit 3   39

Review

A. Vocabulary. Complete each sentence. Write the words on the line.

1. My car won't start. I need a _____.
   _{tow truck / pickup truck}

2. There's a problem with the _____. I can't close it.
   _{engine / trunk}

3. It's a good idea to _____ the oil when you buy gas.
   _{remove / check}

B. Conversation. Choose <u>your</u> response. Circle the letter.

1. "Can you bring it in today?"
   a. Sure. What time?
   b. Yes. I can leave it here.

2. "Can she leave it a while?"
   a. I think so. I'll check.
   b. Next to the exit door.

3. "It'll be about $200."
   a. Can you give me an estimate?
   b. That's a lot. I'll have to think about it.

C. Grammar. Put the underlined words in order. Write each sentence on the line.

1. We dropped our car off this morning. <u>pick / What time / up / it / we / can /?</u>

   _____

2. Her headlights aren't working. <u>on / She / them / can't / turn / .</u>

   _____

D. Grammar. Choose the past continuous or the simple past tense. Circle the verb.

Dear Lisa:

It <u>rained / was raining</u> yesterday, and I <u>drove / was driving</u> my old pickup truck.
      1.   2.
At 3:00 my problems <u>started / were starting</u>. The windshield wipers
                         3.
<u>stopped / were stopping</u>, and I couldn't see. And then the oil pressure warning
     4.
light <u>went on / was going on</u>. The owner's manual for the truck <u>said / was saying</u>
       5.   6.
to stop right away. While I <u>read / was reading</u> the manual, a friend
                              7.
<u>saw / was seeing</u> me. That was lucky! She <u>drove / was driving</u> me to a telephone,
   8.   9.
and I <u>called / was calling</u> a tow truck. What a day!
         10.

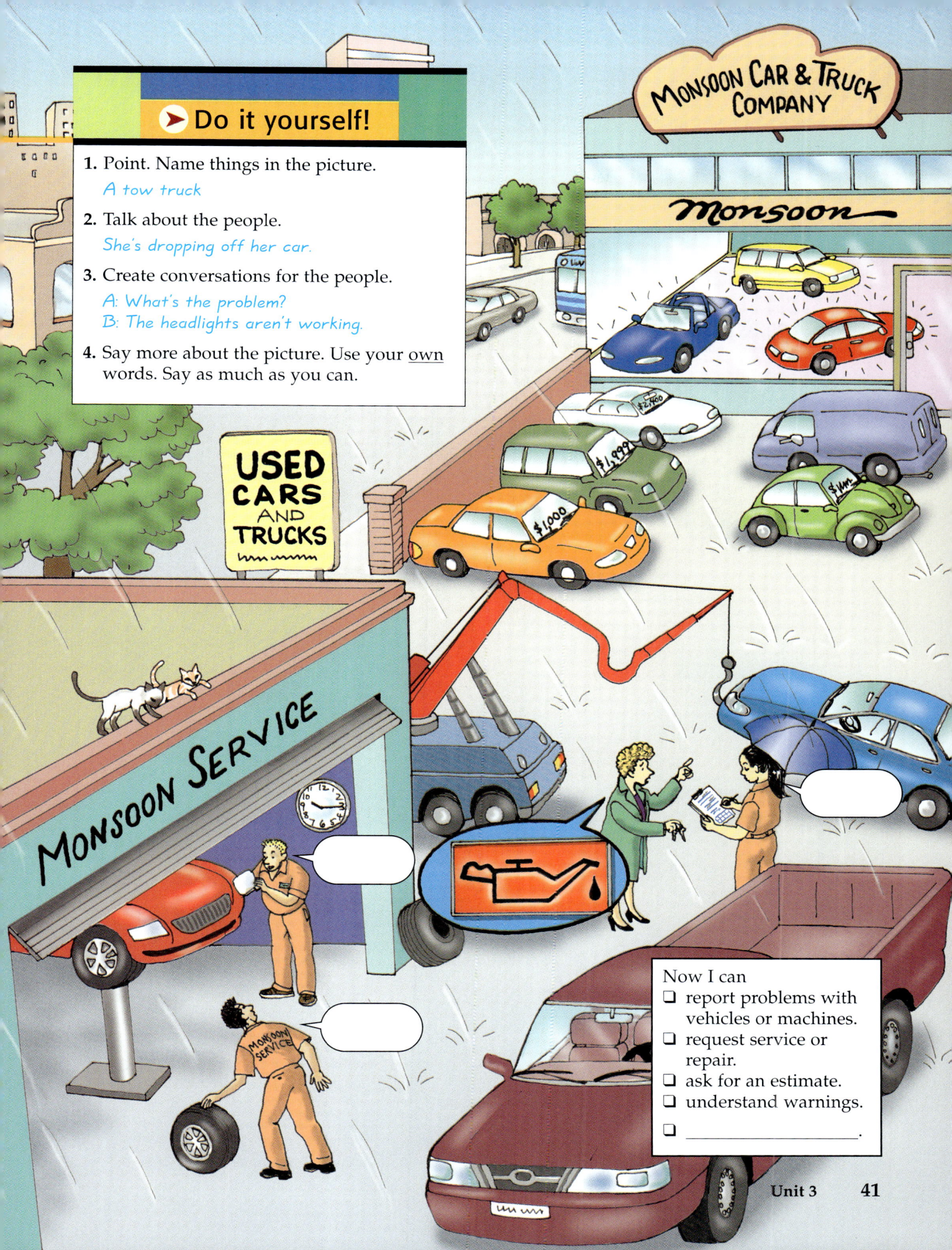

UNIT 4

The consumer world

Vocabulary

Objectives
- talk about personal care products and medicines
- request and offer a rain check
- discuss an overcharge

Picture dictionary

A. Listen.

Personal care products
1. soap
2. shampoo
3. toothpaste
4. a toothbrush
5. deodorant
6. a comb
7. a brush
8. a thermometer
9. tissues

Medicines
10. painkillers
11. cough medicine

Other words
12. a drugstore
13. a camera
14. film
15. a hair dryer
16. a brand
17. a price
18. a sale price
19. dirty
20. clean

42   Unit 4

Personal care

 ㉑ Wash your hair.    ㉒ Brush your hair.    ㉓ Comb your hair.    ㉔ Brush your teeth.

B. Listen again and repeat.

C. Listen to the conversations. Then listen again and match each picture with a conversation. Write the letter on the line.

Conversation 1 _____

Conversation 2 _____

Conversation 3 _____

a.    b. 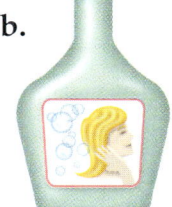   c.

D. Complete each sentence. Write the words on the line.

1. What kind of _____ do you take for a headache? I take aspirin.

painkiller / cough medicine

2. Where's my _____? I want to take a picture of you.

camera / thermometer

3. I have to wash my hair. Do we have any of that great _____?

deodorant / shampoo

4. What brand of _____ do you want for your camera?

tissues / film

5. This brush is _____. I'm going to wash it.

dirty / clean

➤ Do it yourself!

A. Personalization. Make a list of things **you** buy at the drugstore.

B. Pair work. Compare your list with a partner's. Do you buy the same things?

"What do you buy at the drugstore?"

Personal care products	Medicines and other things
1.	1.
2.	2.
3.	3.
4.	4.

Practical conversations

Model 1 Talk about prices.

A. Listen and read.

A: I'm looking for a hair dryer. How much is the one over here?
B: Which one?
A: The red one.
B: $24.99.
A: Do you have any cheaper ones?
B: Yes. And they're on sale. They're only $9.99. They're usually $14.99.

B. Listen again and repeat.

C. Pair work. Now use the pictures or your <u>own</u> words.

A: I'm looking for _____. How much is the one over here?
B: Which one?
A: The _____ one.
B: $ _____.
A: Do you have any cheaper ones?
B: Yes. And they're on sale. They're only _____. They're usually _____.

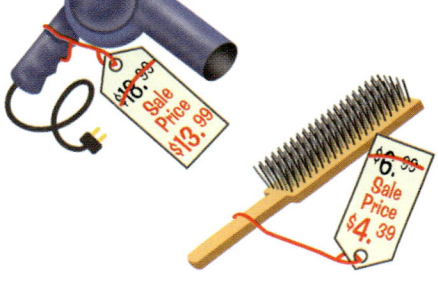

Model 2 Ask for a rain check.

A. Listen and read.

A: That'll be $7.21, please.
B: But this film's on sale for $4.99.
A: I'm sorry, but that price is for the store brand. And we're sold out.
B: That's too bad. Will you give me a rain check?
A: No problem. Here you go. It's good for a month.

B. Listen again and repeat.

RAIN CHECK • GOOD FOR ONE MONTH •
Item sold out: <u>Discount Drugs brand film</u>
Price: <u>sale price $4.99</u>
Date: <u>June 6</u>

C. Pair work. Now use the pictures or your <u>own</u> words.

A: That'll be $ _____, please.
B: But this _____'s on sale for $ _____.
A: I'm sorry, but that price is for the store brand. And we're sold out.
B: That's too bad. Will you give me a rain check?
A: _____. Here you go. It's good for _____.

Model 3 Talk about an overcharge. Offer to correct it.

A. Listen and read.

A: Excuse me. I think I was overcharged. This shampoo's on sale.
B: Oh, I'm sorry. Let me have a look.
A: See, it says "Special $1.99."
B: Yes, you're right. I'll ring it up again.

B. Listen again and repeat.

C. Pair work. Now use your <u>own</u> words.

A: Excuse me. I think I was overcharged. This _____'s on sale.
B: Oh, I'm sorry. Let me have a look.
A: See, it says "_____."
B: _____. I'll ring it up again.

▶ Do it yourself!

Pair work. Create a conversation for the people in the picture. Use your <u>own</u> words.

Practical grammar

A. Complete each sentence with the comparative form of the adjective.

1. Is Clean Skin soap ____better____ than the store brand?
   good
2. Our camera is _____ than their camera.
   new
3. Today's weather is _____ than yesterday's weather!
   bad
4. A computer is usually _____ than a cash register.
   expensive
5. Are the cashiers _____ today than they were yesterday?
   busy

B. Write comparisons with the words.

1. Bell Food Store is / cheap / Quickway
   Bell Food Store is cheaper than Quickway.
2. My new camera is / large / my old camera
   _____

46   Unit 4

3. Discount Drugs is / clean / Quickway

_____

4. The large hair dryers are / expensive / the small hair dryers

_____

5. Today's weather is / hot / yesterday's weather

_____

One / ones and questions with Which

Which toothbrush do you want? — The red one.
Which one? — The one over there.

And which tissues do you want? — The cheap ones.
Which ones? — The ones on that shelf. Next to the aspirin.

C. Complete each conversation with Which, one, or ones.

1. A: *Which* comb did you buy?
   B: The black one.

2. A: _____ toothbrushes do you like?
   B: I like the cheaper ones.

3. A: _____ deodorant is on sale?
   B: The larger one.

4. A: Is she buying the red cough medicine?
   B: No, she's buying the orange _____.

5. A: Do they like these new thermometers?
   B: No. They like the old _____.

6. A: Which tissues do you want?
   B: The _____ over there.

7. A: Why did you sell your old camera?
   B: I bought a better _____.

8. A: Why did you use this shampoo?
   B: Because it's better than that _____.

▶ Do it yourself!

A. Personalization. Complete the chart with three things you buy at the drugstore.

B. Pair work. Compare brands.

Is So Soft soap cheaper than Perfect Skin soap?

Yes, I think so. But Perfect Skin soap is better.

Product	Brand	Adjective
soap	So Soft	cheap
1.		
2.		
3.		

Unit 4   47

Authentic practice 1

With words you know, YOU can talk to this customer.

A. Listen and read.

Customer: Excuse me. Do you work here?
YOU: Yes. I'm the assistant manager. Can I help you?
Customer: I hope so. I bought this here last Saturday, but there's something wrong with it.
YOU: Oh, that's too bad. What's wrong?
Customer: The film compartment won't close. Can I exchange it?
YOU: I'm sorry. We're sold out right now. Would you like a rain check?
Customer: Well, that's very nice of you, but I think I'd like to have another brand. How much are those?
YOU: Well, those are on sale—only $20. And they're better than this one, I think.
Customer: Terrific. I'll take one.

B. Listen to the customer. Read your part out loud.

C. Listen and read. Choose your response. Circle the letter.

1. "Excuse me. Do you work here?"
   a. No, I'm sorry, I don't.   b. It doesn't work. I want to exchange it.
2. "There's something wrong with this camera."
   a. OK, I'll ring it up again.   b. Oh, what's wrong with it?
3. "I'd like to exchange this for one that's on sale."
   a. Sure. We're sold out.   b. Fine. We have one for only $10.00.
4. "How much is this soap?"
   a. I'll take three boxes.   b. It's on sale for $1.29.
5. "I'll take one."
   a. Here you go.   b. That's too bad.

48   Unit 4

🎧 **D.** Listen. Choose your response. Circle the letter.

1. a. No problem.   b. No. It's too expensive.
2. a. Two months.   b. We're sold out.
3. a. I can give you a rain check.   b. Let me look at your receipt.

Listening comprehension

🎧 **A.** Listen to the announcement. Then answer the questions. Circle the letter.

1. Who is the speaker?
   a. an announcer on the radio   b. a customer of 77 Electronics
2. What is 77 Electronics?
   a. a brand of camera   b. a store
3. What is the speaker talking about?
   a. a copy shop   b. a sale

🎧 **B.** Look at the chart. Then listen again for the price of each item. Write the prices on the chart.

🎧 **C.** In your own words. Listen again.

What would you like to buy at 77 Electronics?

_____

Tell your partner why.

Item	Price
Perfect Picture camera	$ 27.77
Brew Right coffee maker	
Copy Clean home copier	
copier paper	
computer diskettes	
pocket calendar	

▸ Do it yourself!

A. Write your own response. Then read your conversation out loud with a partner.

Excuse me. Do you work here?
YOU _____

I have a problem.
YOU _____

I think I was overcharged for this camera.
YOU _____

B. Personalization. Talk about a sale in your neighborhood.

Authentic practice 2

Reading

A. Read the ad. Check ☑ the items that are on sale.

- ❏ screwdrivers
- ❏ pliers
- ❏ drills
- ❏ saws
- ❏ goggles
- ❏ batteries

B. Critical thinking. Read about these Tool Box customers. Choose the correct response.

> Yes, you're right. I'll ring that up for you again.

> No, I'm sorry. That is the right price.

Walker

1. On Monday, Ms. Walker paid $2.99 for an 8' vinyl tape measure. She said to the cashier, "I think I was overcharged."

   Response: _____

Reyes

2. Ms. Reyes bought a 15" Rapid Cut saw on Tuesday. She paid $14.39. She checked her receipt and said to the cashier, "I think I was overcharged."

   Response: _____

Cheng

3. Mr. Cheng bought a Tool Box power drill on Wednesday. He paid $59.99. He said to the cashier, "I think I was overcharged."

   Response: _____

Writing

A. Look at the ad on page 50 again. Then look at the rain check from the Tool Box. Answer the question.

Late Monday afternoon, the power drills were sold out, so customers got rain checks. How long is the rain check good for? _____

The Tool Box — Rain Check
Date _September 18_
Sold-out item _Tool Box power drill_
Sale price _$42.99_
Good until _October 18_

B. Collaborative activity. Create a conversation. It's Tuesday afternoon at the Tool Box. The power drills and the 26" saws are sold out.

Partner A, you are a customer. You want to buy a 26" saw. Ask Partner B for a rain check.

Partner B, you are a cashier. Fill out a rain check for Partner A.

The Tool Box — Rain Check
Date _____
Sold-out item _____
Sale price _____
Good until _____

For extra practice, go to page 142.

▶ Do it yourself!   A plan-ahead project

Discussion. Bring in ads from the newspaper or from stores in your neighborhood. Compare your ads.

Perfect Picture cameras are on sale at Discount Drugs for $19.99.

Unit 4   51

Review

A. Vocabulary. Complete each sentence. Write the words on the line.

1. I'll be ready in a minute. I just have to _____ my teeth.

brush / comb

2. I washed my hair with this _____, but I don't like it.

toothpaste / shampoo

3. My hair is _____. I have to wash it.

clean / dirty

B. Conversation. Choose <u>your</u> response. Circle the letter.

1. "We're sold out."
   - a. Oh, that's too bad.
   - b. Is it good for a month?

2. "Excuse me. I think I was overcharged."
   - a. OK. I'll give you a rain check.
   - b. Let me have a look at the price.

3. "I'm sorry. I'll ring it up again."
   - a. Thanks.
   - b. That's worse.

C. Grammar. Complete each sentence with <u>one</u> or <u>ones</u>.

1. I need a new camera. How much is this _____?
2. Which toothbrushes are on sale? The _____ on the shelf?
3. Do you want these tissues or the _____ over there?

D. Grammar. Write comparisons with the words.

1. The Efficiency saw is / good / the Tool Box saw

   _____

2. I am / busy / my manager

   _____

E. Reading and writing. Read the ad. Then fill out a rain check for one of the products.

52   Unit 4

UNIT 5

Time

Vocabulary

Picture dictionary

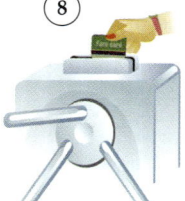

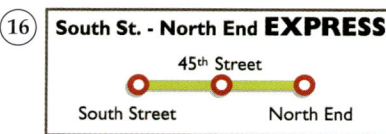

Objectives
- ask about schedules
- explain lateness
- read bus and train schedules
- buy tickets and pay fares

A. Listen.

Transportation and commuting

1. leave
2. arrive
3. take a bus
4. take a train
5. take a taxi
6. buy a ticket
7. buy a token
8. use a fare card
9. miss the bus
10. have a flat tire
11. be stuck in traffic
12. run out of gas
13. the fare
14. one way
15. round trip
16. the express
17. the local

Other words

18. before
19. after

Ways to say the time

  three ten
ten after three
ten after
ten past three
ten past

 three fifteen
a quarter after three
a quarter after
a quarter past three
a quarter past

How to say it

present	past
leave	left
take	took
buy	bought
have	had
be	was / were

 three thirty
half past three
half past

 three forty-five
a quarter to four
a quarter to

B. Listen again and repeat.

C. Listen to the conversations. Then listen again and match each clock with a conversation. Write the letter on the line.

a.   b.  c.  d.  e.

1. _____   2. _____   3. _____   4. _____   5. _____

D. Complete the paragraph with words from the box.

took   missed   had   fare   bought   arrived   stuck in traffic   one-way ticket

What a day! First I was _____ for 20 minutes and then I
                              1.
_____ a flat tire! I _____ the 8:00 train, so I _____ the 9:35.
    2.   3.   4.
The round-trip _____ is $6.00. I had only $5.00, so I _____
                    5.   6.
a _____. I _____ at work at 10:30 — one and a half hours late.
        7.   8.

▶ Do it yourself!

A. Personalization. What public transportation do you use? Complete the chart.

B. Discussion. Talk about the public transportation in your city or town. Is it good or bad? Expensive or cheap?

	Fare	Fare card, token, ticket, or cash?
bus	$1.50	fare card
bus		
subway		
train		

I take the subway to work. It's cheap, but it's dirty.

Practical conversations

Model 1 Buy a ticket.

A. Listen and read.

A: One ticket to San Pedro, please.
B: Round trip or one way?
A: Round trip. What's the fare?
B: $2.50.
A: Here you go. When's the next train?
B: In 10 minutes. At 8:15.

B. Listen again and repeat.

C. Pair work. Now use the clock and the schedule and your <u>own</u> words.

A: _____ to _____, please.
B: Round trip or one way?
A: _____. What's the fare?
B: _____.
A: Here you go. When's the next train?
B: In _____ minutes. At _____.

FROM DENSON TO SAN PEDRO
Monday to Friday

FARE	Denson - Carson	$3.85
	Denson - San Pedro	$4.25

LEAVE	ARRIVE	ARRIVE
Denson	Carson	San Pedro
5:12	5:24	5:31
5:22	5:34	5:41
5:32	5:44	5:51

Model 2 Ask about a bus or a train.

A. Listen and read.

A: Did the bus to Pleasantville leave yet?
B: Yes. You just missed it. It left five minutes ago.
A: Oh, no. When's the next one?
B: Well, they leave every 15 minutes, so you could take the 3:15.

B. Listen again and repeat.

C. Pair work. Invent a bus or train to your own city or town.

A: Did the _____ to _____ leave yet?
B: Yes. You just missed it. It left _____ ago.
A: Oh, no. When's the next one?
B: Well, they leave every _____, so you could take the _____.

Model 3   Ask if you're too late.

A. Listen and read.

A: Can I still make the 5:22?
B: Yes. It's still here. Do you need a ticket?
A: No, I already have one.
B: It's leaving soon. You should hurry.

B. Listen again and repeat.

C. Pair work. Now use the schedule and your own words.

A: Can I still make the _____?
B: Yes. It's still here. Do you need a ticket?
A: _____.
B: It's leaving _____. You should hurry.

LEAVES	ARRIVES
9:05	10:00
9:15	10:10
9:25	10:20

▸ Do it yourself!

Pair work. Create a conversation for the people in the picture. Use your own words.

Practical grammar

Should

Should I take the 5:12?   No, you shouldn't. You should take the 4:59.
Should he buy a one-way ticket? Yes, he should.
When should I arrive?   How about ten to three?

A. Complete each sentence with a form of should and the verb.

1. He _should take_ the express. The local arrives too late.
   _{take}

2. You _____ early tonight. There's a lot of traffic.
   _{leave}

3. Which bus _____ we _____?
   _{take}

4. Where _____ I _____ a token?
   _{buy}

5. We _____ him before noon. He's very busy.
   _{call}

6. You _____ the express. It doesn't stop at 79th Street.
   _{not take}

7. Should they drive? No, they _____. They'll get stuck in traffic.
   _{should not}

Could

Could I take the train?   The train already left, but you could take a taxi.
Could we take the bus?   No, you couldn't. It doesn't stop there.

58   Unit 5

B. Complete the conversations. Use a form of could and the verb.

Did the 7:55 express leave yet?

Yes, but you _____ (1. take) the local. It leaves at 8:03.

Bob missed the school bus again. What should we do?

Well, we _____ (2. drive) him to school. Or he _____ (3. walk)!

Which trains _____ we _____ (4. take) to get there before 6:00?

Well, we _____ (5. take) the 5:35 local.

No, we _____ (6. could not). It'll arrive too late. But look! We still _____ (7. make) the 5:22 express.

You're right. But we should hurry. It's leaving soon.

Do it yourself!

Pair work. Linda and Edward Kim are at Central Station. They work in Oak Plains. Work begins at 9:00. They have to arrive before 9:00 to be on time for work.
What trains could they take? What train should they take? Talk with a partner.

The Kims

CARMEL LINE
Blue numbers = Express trains

Cent. Sta.	Northway	Hot Springs	Oak Plains	Carmel
7:15	7:30	8:00	8:30	9:00
7:25	7:40	--------	8:25	8:55
7:30	--------	8:05	--------	8:55
7:30	7:45	8:15	8:45	9:15
7:50	8:05	8:35	9:05	9:35

Authentic practice 1

With words you know, YOU can talk to this supervisor.

🎧 **A. Listen and read.**

Supervisor:	Martina Loyola.
YOU	Ms. Loyola? Hi, this is Erika Bender. I'm sorry. I'm going to be late today.
Supervisor:	Are you OK, Erika? What's wrong?
YOU	Well, I had a flat tire. Then I missed my train. It left five minutes ago.
Supervisor:	That's too bad. I'm afraid you might miss the computer training class. It starts at nine sharp and it's already twenty to. You should take a taxi.
YOU	Excuse me?
Supervisor:	Could you take a taxi? It's already twenty minutes to nine.
YOU	Yes, I could.
Supervisor:	Good. Well, thanks for calling, Erika. Please hurry in.
YOU	OK, Ms. Loyola. See you soon.

🎧 **B. Listen to the supervisor. Read your part out loud.**

🎧 **C. Listen and read. Choose your response. Circle the letter.**

1. "I'm afraid you might miss the 7:18."
   - a. That's good.
   - b. When's the next one?

2. "The train leaves at 9:45 sharp."
   - a. We should hurry.
   - b. Round trip or one way?

3. "I'm afraid you just missed the meeting."
   - a. Oh, no!
   - b. It already left.

🎧 **D. Listen. Choose your response. Circle the letter.**

1. a. What's the problem? b. Patrick? Hi.
2. a. I just missed it. b. Yes. I'll take the next train.
3. a. OK. Thanks. b. Oh, no. Did I miss it?

Listening comprehension

A. Listen to the conversation. Then answer the questions. Circle the letter.

1. Who are the people?
   a. A delivery driver and a customer.
   b. A delivery driver and a co-worker.
2. What's the problem?
   a. A driver's stuck in traffic.
   b. A driver's going to be late.

B. Listen again for the times. Circle the times.

1. What time is it? 6:30 6:45 7:00 7:15
2. What time does Daniel's shift usually start? 6:30 6:45 7:00 7:15
3. When will Miguel arrive at the Full Moon Diner? 6:30 6:45 7:00 7:15

C. Critical thinking. Now listen again. When did the truck arrive at the company? Circle the time. 6:30 6:45 7:00 7:15

D. In your own words. Listen again. Answer the question and then talk with a partner.

What is Daniel going to do? _____

➤ Do it yourself!

A. Write your own response. Then read your conversation out loud with a partner.

It's already twenty after nine. You're really late. Where are you?
YOU _____

Are you OK? What happened?
YOU _____

Could you still get here before eleven?
YOU _____

B. Personalization. Talk about a problem you had going to work or class.

Authentic practice 2

Reading

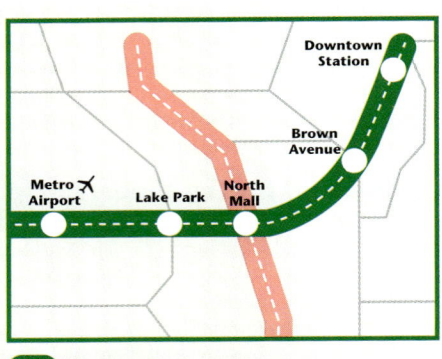

RAPID Transit Schedule

State Street Line

Monday through Friday
Metro Airport to Downtown Station
E Express trains do <u>not</u> stop at Lake Park or Brown Avenue.

Metro Airport	Lake Park	North Mall	Brown Avenue	Downtown Station
6:26	6:33	6:42	6:53	7:09
E 6:53	X	7:06	X	7:27
7:06	7:12	7:22	7:33	7:50
E 7:17	X	7:30	X	7:51
7:27	7:34	7:43	7:54	8:11

A. Look at the schedule. What are the stops on the State Street Line? _____

_____

B. Critical thinking. Now read about the workers. Answer the questions. Circle the letter.

Hong

1. Jack Hong took the 7:12 from Lake Park. What time will he arrive at North Mall?

   a. 7:06 **b.** 7:22 **c.** 7:33

Kibit

2. Barbara Kibit is at Brown Avenue at 7:30. She needs to arrive at Downtown Station before 8:00. Which train should she take?

   a. the 7:22 **b.** the 7:33 **c.** the 7:54

Salinas

3. It is 6:30. David Salinas is at the Metro Airport station. He missed the 6:26. He needs to go to Brown Avenue. What is the next train he could take?

   a. the 6:26 **b.** the 7:06 **c.** the 6:53

Torres

4. Rita Torres lives near Lake Park. She needs to arrive at Downtown Station before 8:00. Which trains could she take?

   a. the 6:33 or 7:12 **b.** the 6:33 or 7:17 **c.** the 7:12 or 7:34

Writing

A. Listen. Where does the customer want to go? Circle the letter.

a. Los Angeles   b. Rialto

B. Mario, Laura, and Hans have to go to a computer training class in Rialto. They can't leave before 7:30 a.m. They have to arrive before 10:00 a.m.

Listen to the announcement again. Write the departure and arrival times of trains they could take.

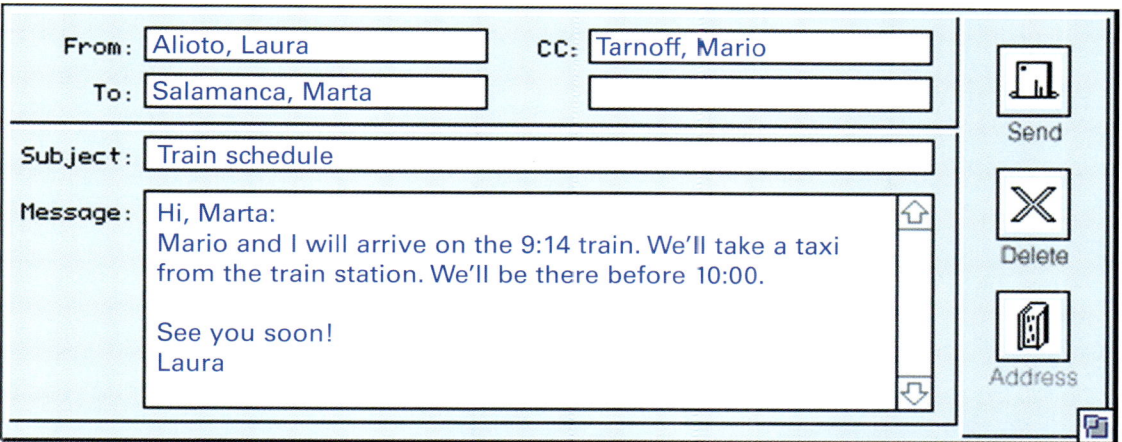

Leaves   Arrives

C. Mario and Laura decide to take the first possible train. Read the e-mail message to their supervisor.

From:	Alioto, Laura	CC:	Tarnoff, Mario
To:	Salamanca, Marta		
Subject:	Train schedule		
Message:	Hi, Marta: Mario and I will arrive on the 9:14 train. We'll take a taxi from the train station. We'll be there before 10:00. See you soon! Laura		

Hans has to take a later train. Choose a train for Hans. Complete his e-mail message.

From:	Gottsman, Hans	CC:	Tarnoff, Mario; Alioto, Laura
To:	Salamanca, Marta		
Subject:	Train schedule		
Message:	Hi, Marta: Hans		

For extra practice, go to page 143.

▶ Do it yourself!   A plan-ahead project

Collaborative activity. Bring in a train or bus schedule. Choose a place. Make plans to go there. You have to return home before 5:30. Which trains or buses can you take?

Unit 5   63

Review

A. Vocabulary. Complete each sentence. Write the words on the line.

1. I missed the _____. When is the next local?
   _{express / fare}
2. I'd like a _____ ticket. I don't have enough money for a round trip.
   _{local / one-way}
3. Please arrive _____ 4:00. The meeting starts at 4:00 sharp.
   _{after / before}

B. Vocabulary. Write the time in numbers.

1. Half past eight __8:30__
2. Ten to nine _____
3. Twenty after eight _____
4. A quarter after eight _____

C. Conversation. Choose <u>your</u> response. Circle the letter.

1. "You just missed it."
   a. That's too bad. When's the next one?   b. Is it still here?
2. "You could still make the 6:37. But you should hurry."
   a. Great. Thanks.   b. Well, could I buy a ticket for the 7:42?
3. "Did the 6:37 express leave yet?"
   a. Yes. In ten minutes.   b. Yes. Ten minutes ago.

D. Grammar and reading. Read the bus schedule. Then answer the questions.

Express buses in blue print

Bayville	Walden	Beacon	Salem
6:00	6:25	6:55	7:00
6:10	X	6:55	7:00
6:15	X	7:00	7:05
6:20	6:45	7:15	7:20
6:20	X	7:05	7:10

1. When does the first express bus leave Bayville? _____
2. Katerina Valenti wants to arrive in Salem before 7:15. Which bus should she take from Walden? _____
3. Ali Petak wants to arrive in Salem before 7:15. Which buses could he take from Bayville? _____

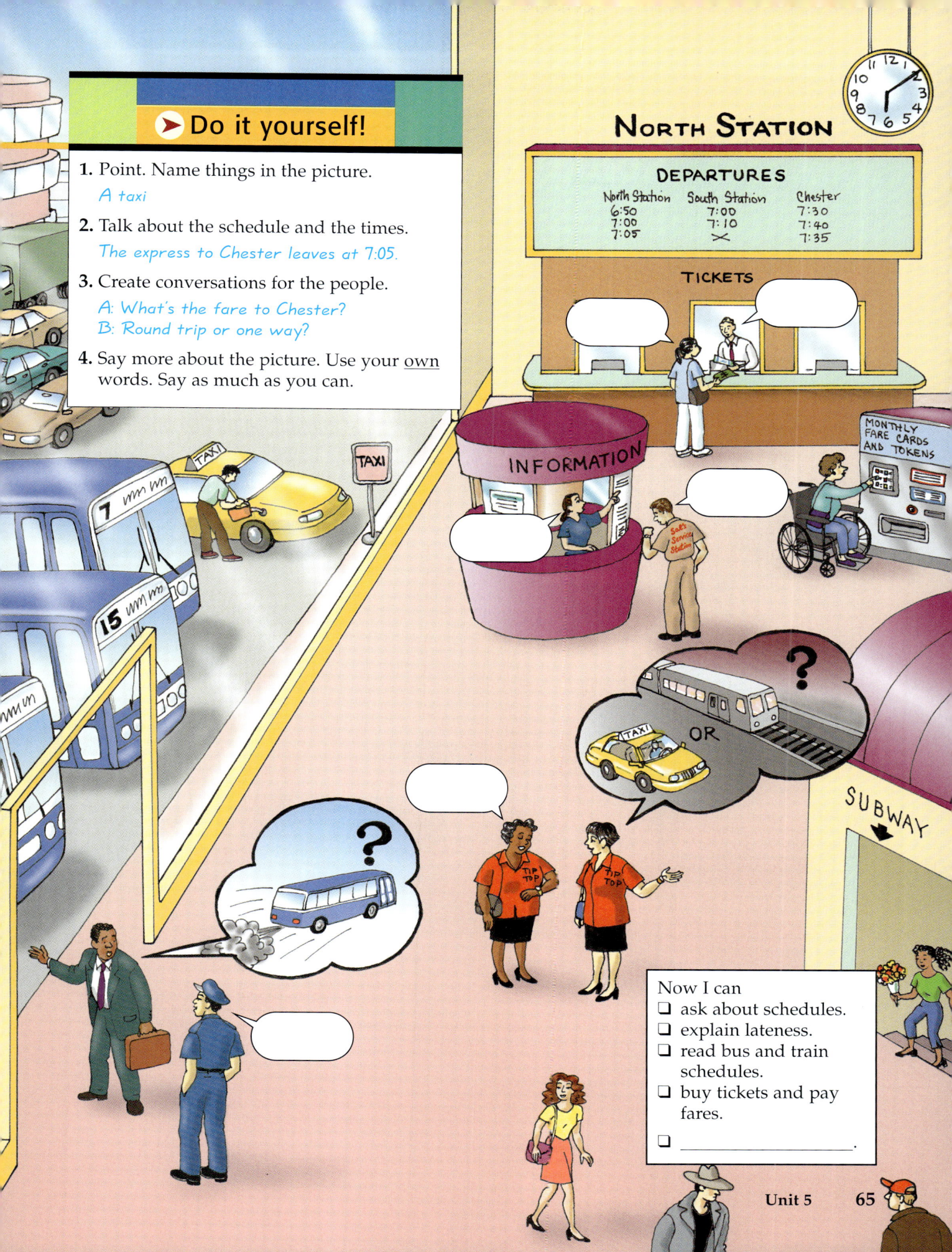

UNIT 6
Supplies and services

 Vocabulary

Objectives
- ask for help
- offer help
- talk about inventory
- order supplies

Picture dictionary

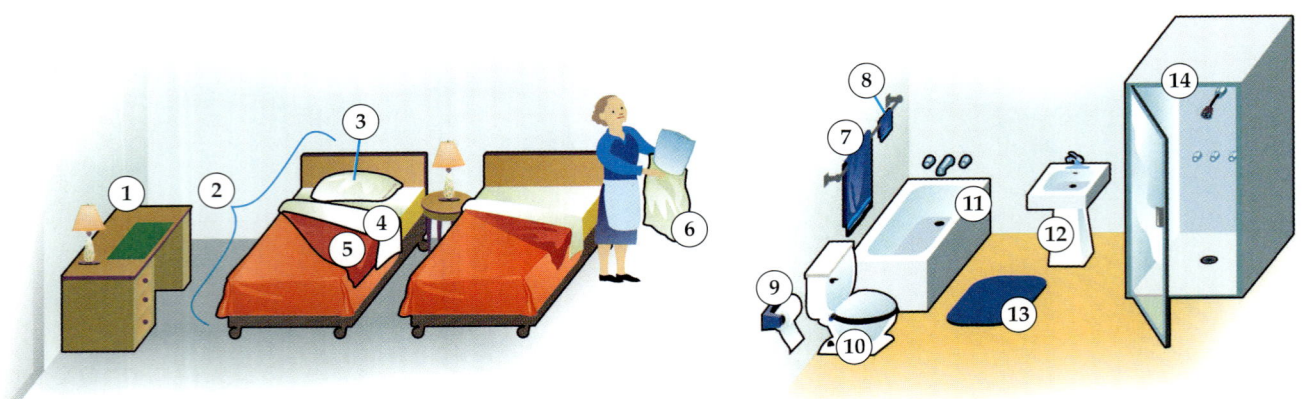

🎧 **A.** Listen.

A bedroom
1. a desk
2. a bed
3. a pillow
4. a sheet
5. a blanket
6. a pillowcase

A bathroom
7. a towel
8. a washcloth
9. toilet paper
10. a toilet
11. a bathtub
12. a sink
13. a bath mat
14. a shower

A supply closet
15. trash bags
16. paper towels
17. a vacuum cleaner
18. a mop
19. a bucket
20. rubber gloves
21. cleansers
22. a sponge
23. furniture polish
24. glass cleaner

Housework

㉕ empty the trash   ㉖ change the sheets   ㉗ make the bed   ㉘ vacuum the carpet   ㉙ do the laundry

🎧 **B.** Listen again and repeat.

🎧 **C.** Listen to the hotel housekeepers. Then listen again and match each picture with a conversation. Write the letter on the line.

Conversation 1 _____   a.    b.    c.

Conversation 2 _____

Conversation 3 _____

D. Complete each sentence. Write the words on the line.

1. All the sheets are dirty. Let's _____ the laundry this afternoon.
   _{make / do}

2. Oh, no. We're out of trash bags, and I have to _____ the trash.
   _{change / empty}

3. I made the beds. Now I have to _____ the carpet.
   _{vacuum / do}

4. Please don't use a paper towel with that cleanser. Use a _____.
   _{pillowcase / sponge}

5. Don't use _____ on the desk; it's for the windows.
   _{glass cleaner / furniture polish}

➤ Do it yourself!

A. Personalization. Complete the chart. Add two cleaning supplies.

B. Discussion. Talk about the products.

Product	Cleans	Room
glass cleaner	windows and mirrors	bathroom, bedroom, kitchen
1.		
2.		

I use Sparkle glass cleaner at home. It cleans windows and mirrors. I use it in the bathroom, the bedroom, and the kitchen.

Unit 6   67

Practical conversations

Model 1 Ask for a favor. Do a favor.

A. Listen and read.

A: Could you please get me some towels from the cart?
B: I'd be glad to. Anything else?
A: No. Thanks for the help. I appreciate it.
B: Anytime.

B. Listen again and repeat.

C. Pair work. Ask for something from a supply room or a cart. Use the pictures or your <u>own</u> words.

A: Could you please get me some _____ from the _____?
B: _____. Anything else?
A: No. Thanks for the help. I appreciate it.
B: _____.

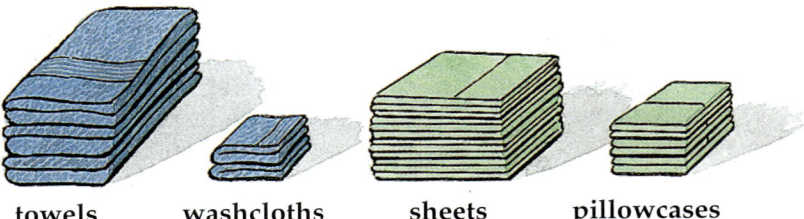

towels   washcloths   sheets   pillowcases

Model 2 Offer to help. Accept or decline the offer.

A. Listen and read.

A: Would you like me to put away the supplies?
B: Oh, thanks for offering, but I can do that myself.
A: Well, please let me know if there's anything I can do.
B: Actually, you could get me a sponge.
A: Sure. No problem.

B. Listen again and repeat.

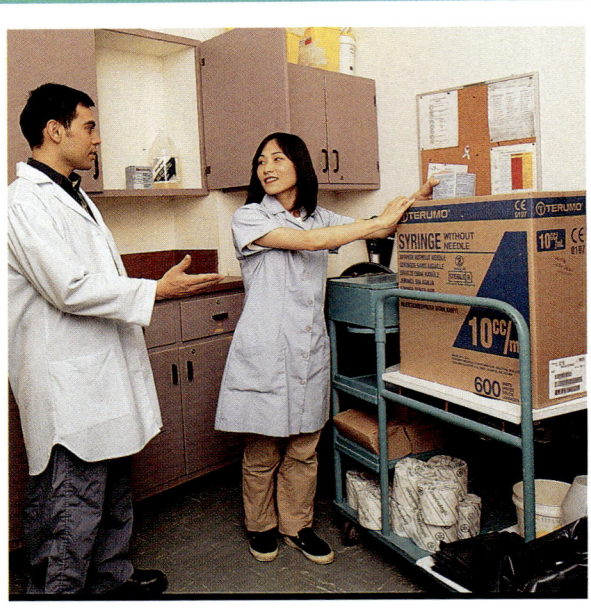

68   Unit 6

C. Pair work. Offer to help. Use the words in the box or your own words.

A: Would you like me to _____?
B: Oh, thanks for offering, but I can do that myself.
A: Well, please let me know if there's anything I can do.
B: Actually, you could get me _____.
A: _____.

> empty the trash
> change the sheets
> clean the bathroom
> vacuum the bedroom

Model 3 Get supplies. Express gratitude.

A. Listen and read.

A: I'm going to the supply room. I need trash bags.
B: Actually, I do too. Could you get me some when you're there?
A: Sure. I'll be right back.
B: Thanks a million.

Supply Checklist
☑ Trash bags
☐ Sponges, large

B. Listen again and repeat.

C. Pair work. Get supplies from a supply room or a cart. Use the pictures or your own words.

A: I'm going to the _____. I need _____.
B: Actually, I do too. Could you get me some when you're there?
A: _____. I'll be right back.
B: _____.

➤ Do it yourself!

Pair work. Create a conversation for the husband and wife. What do they need?

Practical grammar

Agreeing with too and either

affirmative	negative
He's vacuuming the carpet. I am **too**.	She's not working today. I'm not **either**.

A. Read each sentence. Then add a sentence. Use <u>too</u> or <u>either</u>.

1. We like clean bathrooms. (They) _They do too._
2. She has to work tomorrow. (We) _____
3. They need mops. (You) _____
4. He's emptying the trash. (I) _____
5. Tran doesn't see the cart. (I) _I don't either._
6. The plumbers aren't ready. (The electricians) _____
7. She's not making the bed. (He) _____

A / an and the

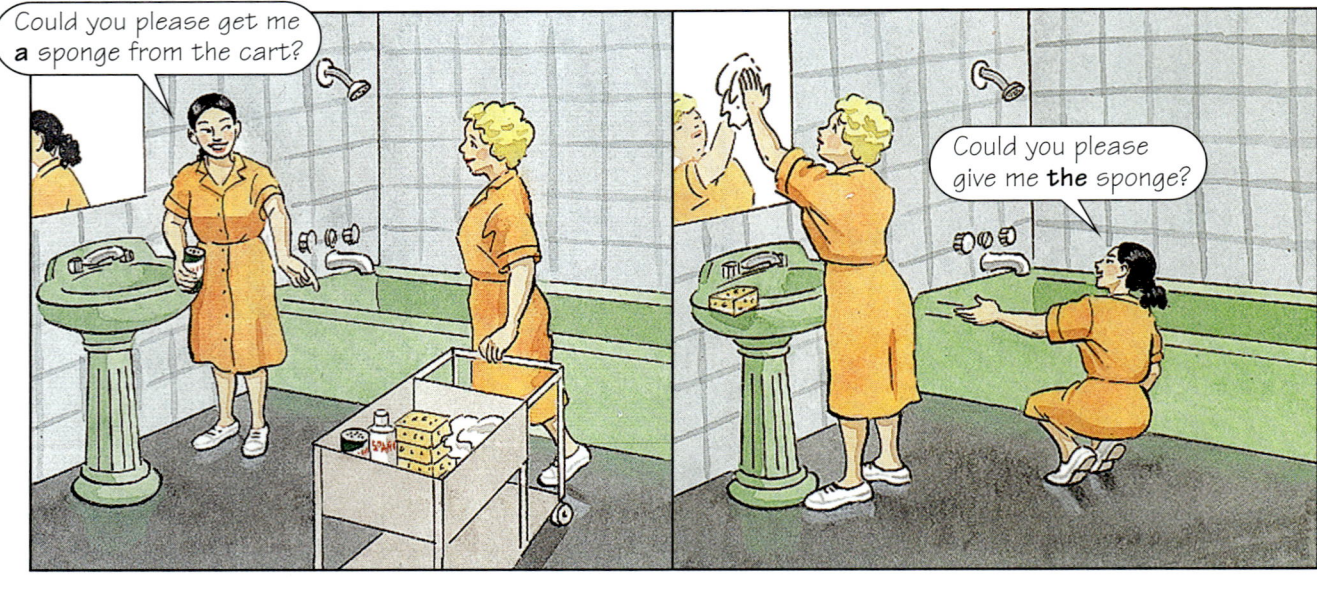

70 Unit 6

B. Look at the pictures. Write <u>a</u>, <u>an</u>, or <u>the</u> on the line.

1. I'm going to get _____ mop.
2. I'm going to get _____ mop.

3. Let's wash _____ window. It's very dirty.
4. I'm looking for _____ apartment.

The present continuous for the future

Use the present continuous to indicate what is happening right now.
　　They**'re changing** the sheets now.

You can also use the present continuous to talk about the future.
　　A: **Are** you **changing** the sheets tomorrow?
　　B: No. We**'re changing** them tonight.

C. Answer the questions about <u>yourself</u>. Use the present continuous.

1. Are you cleaning the halls this afternoon?
   No, I'm cleaning them tomorrow morning.

2. Are you doing the laundry later?
   _____

3. What are you wearing to work tomorrow?
   _____

4. What are you doing next Wednesday night?
   _____

➤ Do it yourself!

Discussion. Talk about your plans for the weekend. Use the pictures or your <u>own</u> plans.

Next Sunday I'm washing the car.

Authentic practice 1

With words you know, YOU can talk to this co-worker.

A. Listen and read.

Co-worker: Hey, I'm so glad you're here.
YOU Why? What's the problem?
Co-worker: Well, the shift is starting in ten minutes, and we're out of practically everything! The guys last night didn't restock.
YOU Is there anything I can do?
Co-worker: Yes. Could you do me a big favor?
YOU Sure.
Co-worker: Would you be nice enough to get some supplies from the stockroom?
YOU I'd be glad to. What do we need?
Co-worker: A couple rolls of paper towels and some furniture polish . . . four or five containers of cleanser and a bunch of clean sponges.
YOU Anything else?
Co-worker: No. I think that's it for now. I don't like starting a shift without the right supplies.
YOU I don't either. I'll be right back.

B. Listen to the co-worker. Read your part out loud.

C. Listen and read. Choose your response. Circle the letter.

1. "Could you do me a big favor?"
   a. Is there anything I can do?   b. Sure.

2. "I'm out of practically everything!"
   a. I'm not either.   b. I am too.

3. "I think that's it for now."
   a. Do you need anything else?   b. Good.

D. Listen. Choose your response. Circle the letter.

1. a. Sure. No problem.   b. Thanks for offering.
2. a. Are you sure?   b. I don't either.
3. a. Thanks. I appreciate it.   b. OK. I'll be right back.

Listening comprehension

A. Listen to the conversation. Then listen again. Write yes or no.

1. Victor and Marie work at the same place. _____
2. Victor and Marie are ordering supplies. _____

B. Listen again. Check ☑ Victor or Marie.

	Victor	Marie
1. Who offers to help?	☐	☐
2. Who accepts help?	☐	☐
3. Who puts away the food?	☐	☐
4. Who puts the laundry in the laundry room?	☐	☐

C. In your own words. Listen again. Answer the questions and then discuss your answers with a partner.

1. What's the problem? _____
   _____

2. How do Victor and Marie solve the problem? _____
   _____

▶ Do it yourself!

A. Write your own response. Then read your conversation out loud with a partner.

I'm so busy today. Would you help me with something?

YOU _____

The supplies are coming in an hour. Could you open the stockroom for me?

YOU _____

I never have enough time!

YOU _____

B. Personalization. Talk about housework. Who does the housework in your house?

Authentic practice 2

Reading

A. Read the supply checklist. Then answer the question.

What are the supplies for? _____

The Wilton Towers
Supply Checklist

Stock the following for each room:

Item	Quantity
mini shampoo	1
mini conditioner	1
body lotion	1
bath soap	1

Item	Quantity
face soap	1
washcloths	2
bath towels	2
face towels	2

Item	Quantity
bath mat	1
flat sheet	1
fitted sheet	1
pillowcases	2

EVERY DAY Change bed linens and towels. Replace personal care products. Empty trash.

B. **Critical thinking.** Alex Palenko is a housekeeper on the third floor of the Wilton Towers Hotel. There are 10 guest rooms. Look at her supply cart. What supplies does she need?

Palenko

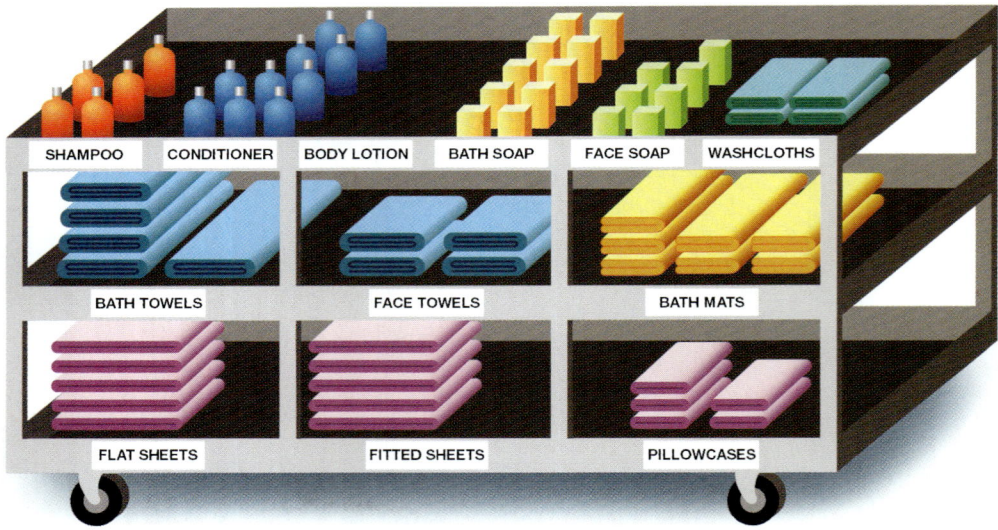

1. __5__ shampoo
2. _____ conditioner
3. _____ body lotion
4. _____ bath soap
5. _____ face soap
6. _____ washcloths
7. _____ bath towels
8. _____ face towels
9. _____ bath mats
10. _____ flat sheets
11. _____ fitted sheets
12. _____ pillowcases

Writing

A. This is the supply room at Metropolitan Hospital. Look at the shelves and the inventory list. Does Ms. Cantu need to order supplies? Write yes or no. _____

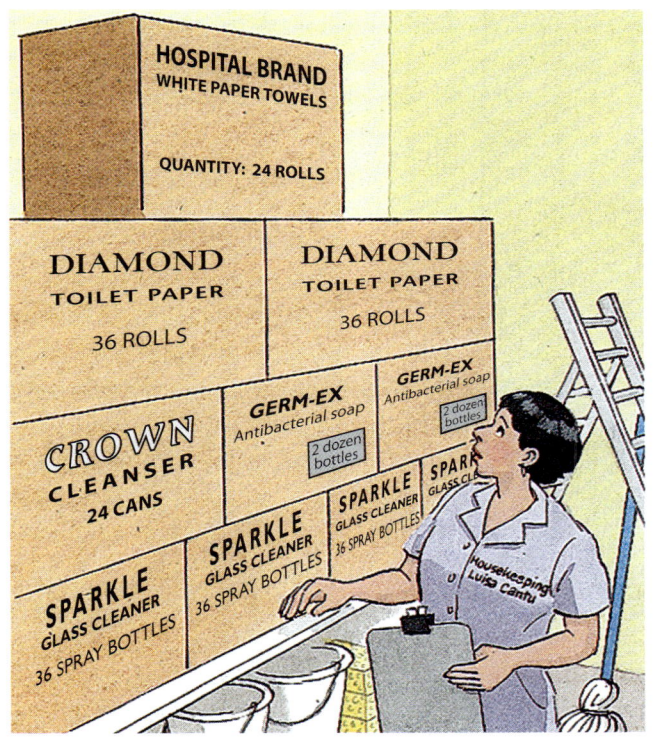

Metropolitan Hospital
22 North Main, Mariposa Valley, TX 78294

Supply Room Inventory
Stock the following items at all times in these quantitites:

ITEM	QUANTITY
paper towels	6 cartons @ 24 rolls each
toilet paper	6 cartons @ 36 rolls each
cleanser, powdered	2 cartons @ 24 cans each
liquid soap	2 cartons @ 2 dozen each
glass cleaner, liquid	5 cartons @ 36 bottles each

B. Fill out the requisition form for the supplies Metropolitan Hospital needs.

Metropolitan Hospital
Central Supply Warehouse
22 North Main, Mariposa Valley, TX 78294

Requisition Form

Today's date: _____

Item	Quantity	Item	Quantity
paper towels	5 cartons		

For extra practice, go to page 144.

▶ Do it yourself!

A. Personalization. What supplies are necessary in a new apartment? On a separate sheet of paper, make lists for the bathroom, the kitchen, and the bedroom.

B. Discussion. Compare lists. Do all the lists contain the same items?

Review

A. Vocabulary. Where do you use these supplies? Write <u>bedroom</u> or <u>bathroom</u>.

1. sheets _____
2. washcloths _____
3. blankets _____
4. bath mat _____
5. toilet paper _____
6. pillows _____

B. Conversation. Choose <u>your</u> response. Circle the letter.

1. "Would you like me to put away the blankets?"
   a. Thanks, but I can do that myself.
   b. Please let me know if there's anything I can do.

2. "Could you please get me some cleanser?"
   a. I appreciate it.
   b. Sure. I'll be right back.

3. "Is there anything I can do to help?"
   a. Let me think.
   b. I'd be glad to.

C. Grammar. Read each sentence. Then add a sentence. Use <u>too</u> or <u>either</u>.

1. "I don't like these pillowcases."
   You: _____

2. "I'm not working tomorrow."
   You: _____

3. "I'm making the beds today."
   You: _____

D. Writing. Complete each answer about <u>yourself</u>.

1. Where are you going tomorrow? *Tomorrow* _____
   _____

2. What are you doing next Saturday? *Next Saturday* _____
   _____

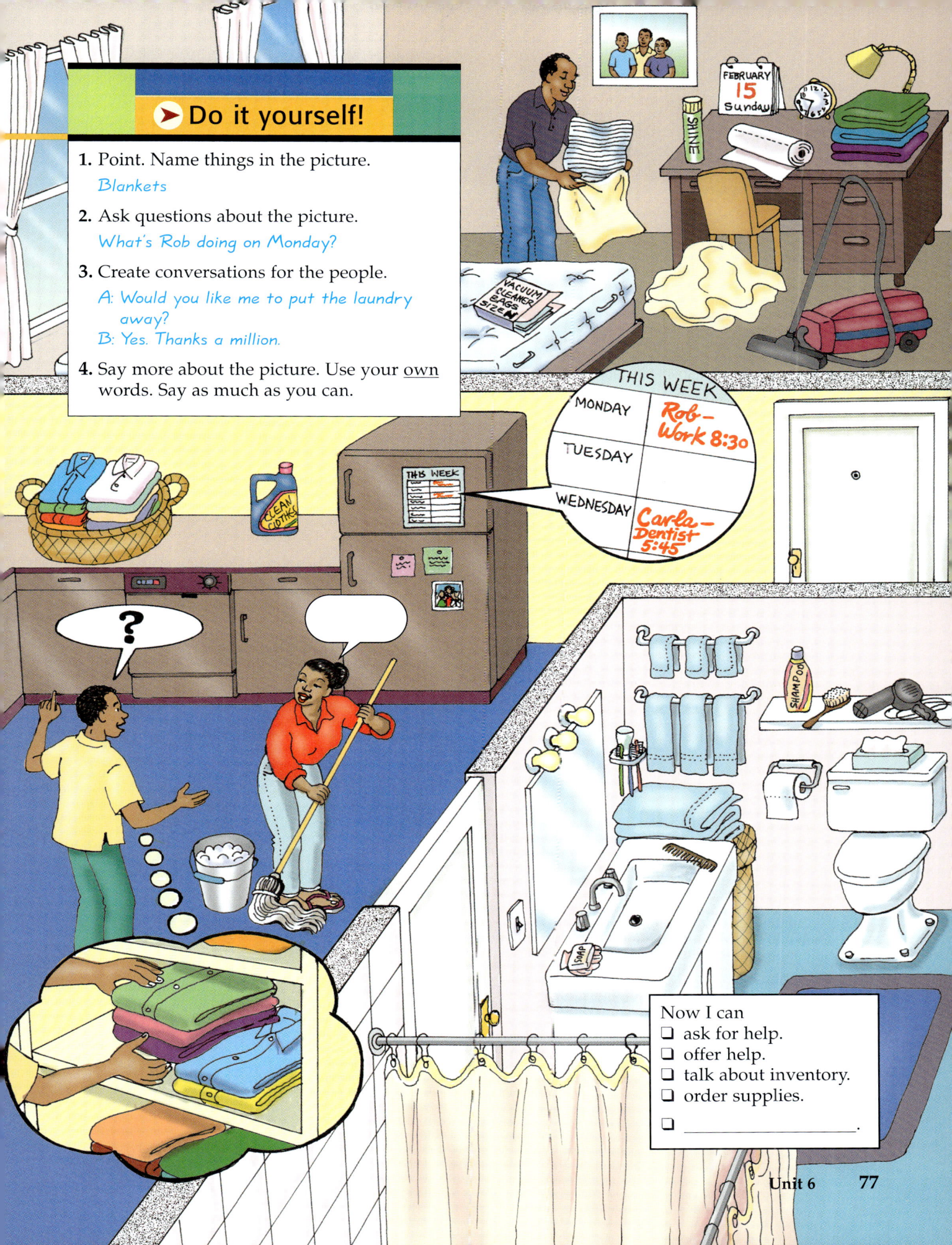

UNIT 7

Relationships

Vocabulary

Objectives
- express preferences
- talk about consequences
- understand procedures

Picture dictionary

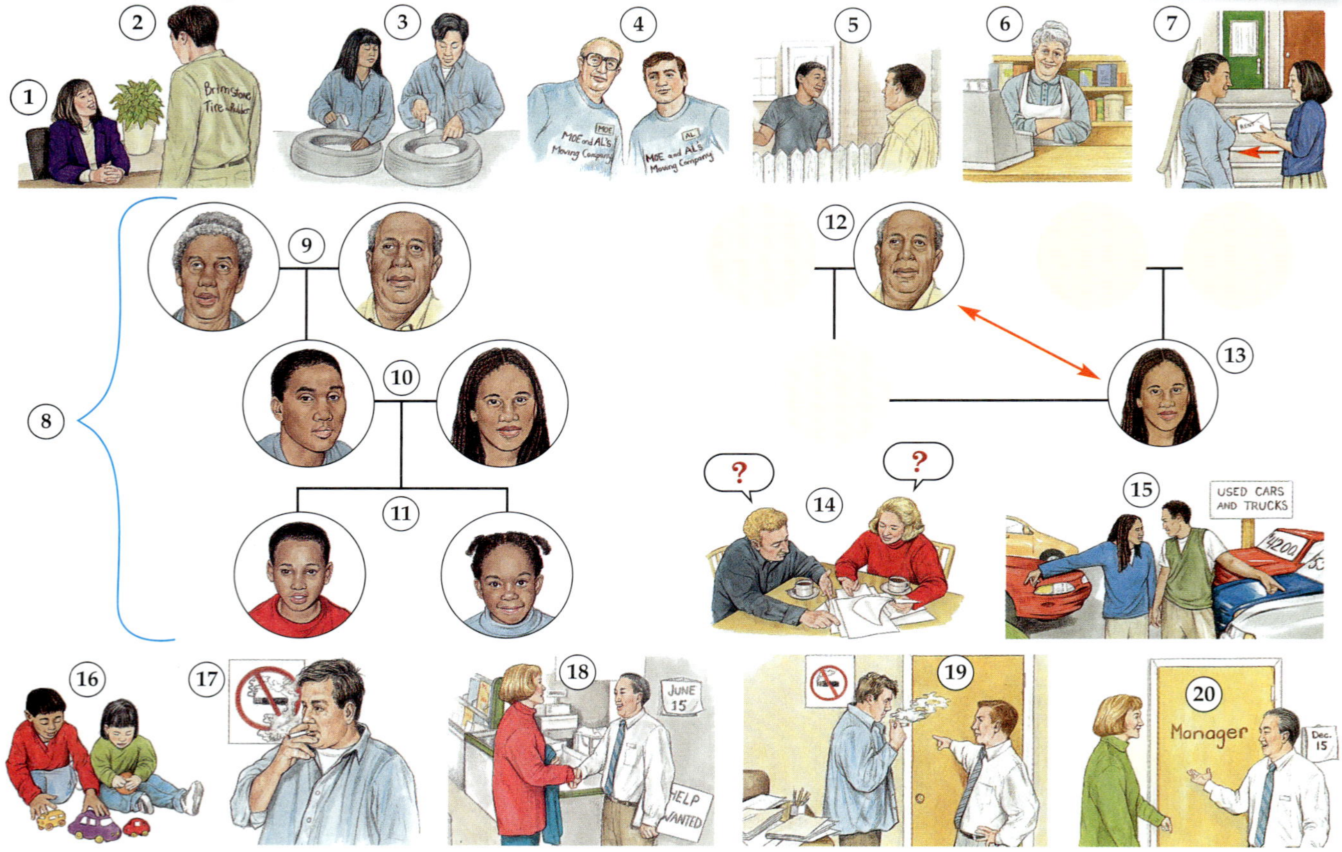

A. Listen.

Work and community relationships
1. an employer
2. an employee
3. co-workers
4. partners
5. neighbors
6. a store owner
7. a landlord

Family relationships
8. relatives
9. grandparents
10. parents
11. children
12. a father-in-law
13. a daughter-in-law

Relating to others
14. discuss a problem
15. disagree
16. get along
17. break the rules
18. get hired
19. get fired
20. get a promotion

78   Unit 7

Other in-law relationships	Other words for "the boss"
a mother-in-law	employer
a son-in-law	supervisor
a sister-in-law	manager
a brother-in-law	owner

B. Listen again and repeat.

C. Listen to the conversations. Then listen again and choose a word or phrase for each conversation.

> discuss a problem   break the rules   get a promotion   disagree

Conversation 1 _____

Conversation 2 _____

Conversation 3 _____

Conversation 4 _____

D. Complete each sentence. Write the words on the line.

1. All my _____ came to dinner last night—my parents, my

neighbors / relatives
   grandparents, and all my sisters and brothers. It was great!

2. The new supervisor started today. He _____ yesterday morning.

got fired / got hired

3. Jan doesn't _____ with her in-laws. They never agree on anything.

get along / disagree

4. This is a big company. It has 200 _____.

employees / relatives

➤ Do it yourself!

A. Personalization. List three people you have a relationship with.

At work	In my family	In my community
Carlos, my boss	Miriam, my daughter-in-law	Fred Lee, my landlord

B. Pair work. Tell your partner about one of the people in your chart. Say as much as you can.

Fred Lee is my landlord. He lives down the street. He gets along with all his neighbors.

Practical conversations

Model 1 Advise someone not to break the rules.

A. Listen and read.

A: I have a question. What will happen if I make a personal call?
B: I'm not sure. But it's against the rules. You'd better not.
A: Really? Well, thanks for telling me.
B: Anytime.

B. Listen again and repeat.

C. Pair work. Ask a partner about the rules. Use the pictures or your <u>own</u> words.

make a personal call

smoke in the building

park in the lot

A: I have a question. What will happen if I _____?
B: _____. But it's against the rules. You'd better not.
A: _____. Well, thanks for telling me.
B: _____.

Model 2 Offer a choice.

A. Listen and read.

A: Would you rather work the day shift or the night shift?
B: That's a good question. I'd better check with my wife.
A: OK. But I need to know soon.
B: Can I tell you tomorrow?
A: Sure. Tomorrow's fine.

B. Listen again and repeat.

How to say it

the day shift / the night shift	the early shift / the late shift
the 7 a.m. shift / the 3 p.m. shift	the first shift / the second shift
from 9 to 5 / from 11 to 3	full-time / part-time

C. Pair work. Agree on a time.

A: Would you rather work _____ or _____?
B: _____. I'd better check with _____.
A: _____. But I need to know soon.
B: Can I tell you _____?
A: Sure. _____'s fine.

Model 3 Discuss a problem. Offer and accept advice.

A. Listen and read.

A: I just don't get along with my in-laws.
B: I'm sorry to hear that. What's the problem?
A: Well, we disagree about money.
B: Maybe if you discuss it with them, you can work it out.
A: I guess it's worth a try.

B. Listen again and repeat.

C. Pair work. Discuss a disagreement. Use the topics in the box or talk about a <u>real</u> disagreement you have with someone.

| money | the children | the rent | the rules |

A: I just don't get along with my _____.
B: I'm sorry to hear that. What's the problem?
A: Well, we disagree about _____.
B: Maybe if you discuss it with _____, you can work it out.
A: I guess it's worth a try.

▶ Do it yourself!

Pair work. Create a conversation for the two men.

Practical grammar

If in statements about the future

*If the weather **is** better tomorrow, we'll **eat** outside.*

***Call** me if you **have** a problem with the computer.*

A. Complete the sentences with the simple present tense.

1. If the weather ____is____ bad, we'll take the bus to work tomorrow.
   (be)
2. If Pedro and his partner _____ about money, they'll have to work it out.
   (disagree)
3. If she _____ the rules again, she won't get that promotion.
   (break)
4. If you _____ the laundry today, please tell your employer.
   (not do)
5. If he _____ with his mother-in-law, tell him to discuss the problem with her.
   (not get along)
6. What will happen if Silvio _____ in the wrong lot?
   (park)
7. Will you get a promotion if you _____ to work late every day?
   (go)
8. Fix the refrigerator if it _____.
   (not work)

B. Complete the sentences with your own words.

1. If you disagree with your in-laws, *discuss the problem with them.*
2. If you take the wrong train, _____
3. If it rains on Saturday, _____

82   Unit 7

Had better

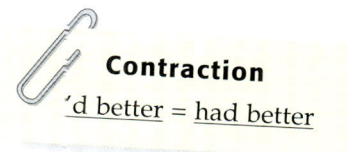

Contraction
'd better = had better

C. Complete each sentence with **'d better** or **had better** and your own words.

1. There's a lot of traffic. She 'd better leave early.
2. It's raining. They _____
3. Martin's supervisor called. Martin _____
4. Martha got fired. She _____

Would rather

D. Pair work. Ask and answer these questions.

1. Would you rather work in an office or at home?
2. Would you rather eat at home or in a restaurant tonight?
3. Would you rather do the laundry or cook dinner?

▶ Do it yourself!

A. Personalization. Complete the questionnaire about yourself.

B. Discussion. Work in a small group. Report your results to the rest of the class.

Two people in our group would rather work the night shift.

Preferences	yes	no	not sure
1. I'd rather work the night shift.	☐	☐	☐
2. I'd rather work part-time.	☐	☐	☐
3. I'd rather work in an office.	☐	☐	☐
4. I'd rather work with my family.	☐	☐	☐

Authentic practice 1

With words you know, YOU can talk to this store owner.

🎧 **A.** Listen and read.

Owner: Good morning, Mr. Tomic. What can I do for you today?

YOU *I have a question. Can you clean this jacket?*

Owner: Let me have a look. Oh, my goodness, what kind of stain is that?

YOU *Stain? Oh . . . it's tomato juice.*

Owner: To tell you the truth, I'm not sure if I can remove that. Maybe, maybe not. I can check. Can you wait a few minutes?

YOU *No. I'd better leave it. I have to go to work.*

Owner: OK. Well, if you call me from work, I'll tell you if I can get the stain out.

YOU *I'm sorry, but I can't make personal calls from work. I'd rather come here after 5:30. Is that OK?*

Owner: Sure, 5:30's fine. But I have to tell you that I might not be able to get it out.

YOU *Well, I like this jacket. It's worth a try.*

🎧 **B.** Listen to the store owner. Read <u>your</u> part out loud.

🎧 **C.** Listen and read. Choose <u>your</u> response. Circle the letter.

1. "What can I do for you today?"
   a. Today's fine.
   b. I have a question. Can I leave this with you?

2. "Maybe I can do it, maybe not."
   a. I'd rather not.
   b. Can you check?

3. "To tell you the truth, I won't be able to fix that."
   a. Thanks for telling me.
   b. Can I tell you later?

🎧 **D.** Listen. Choose <u>your</u> response. Circle the letter.

1. **a.** Is 6:00 OK?   **b.** You'd better not.
2. **a.** It's against the rules. **b.** I'd rather wait.
3. **a.** That's a good idea. **b.** I'd rather check.

Listening comprehension

A. Listen to the speaker. Then complete each sentence. Circle the letter.

1. The woman speaking is _____.
   a. a new employee
   b. a manager

2. The people listening are _____.
   a. new employees
   b. sales managers

B. Read the sentences. Then listen again and check ✓ yes, no, or I don't know.

	yes	no	I don't know
1. New employees are supposed to get folders.	☐	☐	☐
2. Sales managers are supposed to be in the room across the hall.	☐	☐	☐
3. Employees with red folders are supposed to go to the cashier's office.	☐	☐	☐

C. In your own words. Listen again. Answer the questions and then talk with a partner.

1. What kind of meeting is this? _____
2. Who are the people? _____
3. What's the problem? _____

▶ Do it yourself!

A. Write your own response. Then read your conversation out loud with a partner.

Good morning.

YOU _____

What can I do for you today?

YOU _____

To tell you the truth, I'm not sure if I can do that. Can you wait a few minutes?

YOU _____

B. Personalization. Tell your partner about a real conversation you had with a store owner in your neighborhood.

Unit 7

Authentic practice 2

Reading

A. Read the Brimstone Tire and Rubber Company employee manual.

BRIMSTONE Tire and Rubber Company

Benefits for Families of Full-Time Employees

- **Emergency Childcare**
  If your regular childcare arrangements are disrupted and you need to find alternative childcare, Brimstone will provide up to two weeks' childcare at work for employees at the following Brimstone locations: Rubber City and Tulsa. Discuss with your personnel manager.

- **Family Illness or Injury Leave**
  If you have a child, spouse, or parent with a serious illness or injury, Brimstone will provide up to two weeks' time off with full pay to care for the relative or to find care for the relative. Discuss with your personnel manager.

- **Parental Leave (for new parents)**
  If a new child comes into an employee's home by birth, adoption, or foster care placement, Brimstone Tire will allow four weeks of paid parental leave. Additional leave without pay is also available in some situations. Discuss with your personnel manager.

General Rules and Requirements for Family Benefits

- If you know in advance that you will need emergency childcare or family illness or injury leave, please notify your personnel manager and fill out the necessary forms. Brimstone will do everything possible to serve your family in time of need.

- If you need parental leave, you MUST apply for it one month in advance. If you do not apply in advance, leave will automatically be without pay.

B. **Critical thinking.** Read about these Brimstone full-time employees. What benefit can they get? Circle the letter.

Barria

1. Marta Barria is a lathe operator in Tulsa. Her mother was in an accident. Marta needs a nurse's aide to care for her mother at home. She filled out a form the day after the accident. What benefit can Marta Barria get?

   a. parental leave   **b.** no benefit   **c.** family illness or injury leave

Roberts

2. Peter Roberts is a welder in Rubber City. On November 1, 2002, he and his wife adopted a baby girl from Korea. He told his personnel manager one month in advance. What benefit can he get?

   a. no benefit   **b.** parental leave   **c.** emergency childcare

Baraf

3. Yael Baraf works in the Belleville plant. She has four children. Usually Yael's sister-in-law takes care of them, but her sister-in-law is in the hospital and Yael has no childcare right now. She discussed the problem with her personnel manager and filled out a form. What benefit can she get?

   a. no benefit   **b.** emergency childcare   **c.** family illness or injury leave

Writing

Look at Yael Baraf's application for emergency childcare. Then complete an application for Peter Roberts.

BRIMSTONE Tire and Rubber Company
Employee Benefits Application

Today's date: __12__ __2__ __2002__
              month   day   year

Employee name: __Baraf__ __Yael__   Employee work location: __Belleville__
                   last name   first name

Check one: ☑ full-time   ☐ part-time

Benefit applied for (check one)
- ☑ Emergency Childcare
- ☐ Family Illness or Injury Leave
- ☐ Parental Leave

BRIMSTONE Tire and Rubber Company
Employee Benefits Application

Today's date: _____
              month   day   year

Employee name: _____   Employee work location: _____
                   last name   first name

Check one: ☐ full-time   ☐ part-time

Benefit applied for (check one)
- ☐ Emergency Childcare
- ☐ Family Illness or Injury Leave
- ☐ Parental Leave

For extra practice, go to page 145.

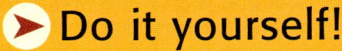 **Do it yourself!**   A plan-ahead project

Discussion. Bring in employee manuals or benefits policies from your job or a relative's job. Or share an employee manual with a classmate. Discuss the policies.

"I get two weeks off with pay every year."

Review

A. Vocabulary. Complete the sentences with words from the box.

| in-laws | landlord | disagree | partner | relatives | promotion |

1. We don't get along. We _____ about everything.
2. Your grandmother and your father-in-law are your _____.
3. She got a _____, and now she's making more money.
4. I always send the rent check to my _____ by the tenth of the month.

B. Conversation. Choose <u>your</u> response. Circle the letter.

1. "What will happen if I break that rule?"
   a. I don't know.   b. I guess it's worth a try.
2. "I'd better check with my partner."
   a. That's fine.   b. I'll tell you tomorrow.
3. "Would you rather tell me tonight or tomorrow?"
   a. I'd better wait until tomorrow.   b. I need to know soon.

C. Grammar. Complete each sentence. Write the words on the line.

1. If you _____ the rules, will you get fired?
   break / will break
2. Please talk to the manager if you _____ parental leave.
   want / will want
3. If you _____ with your relatives, you'll have problems at home.
   won't get along / don't get along

D. Reading and writing. Read about Leonie Lipa. Then read the policy and complete the sentences.

Leonie Lipa works at Atlas Paper. She and her husband are adopting a child from Romania. They have to go there to pick up the baby, and they will have to stay for three weeks to complete the adoption process. Mrs. Lipa wants to take three weeks of parental leave to go to Romania.

Parental Leave Policy

All Atlas Paper employees are entitled to 6 weeks of paid parental leave. Normally, leave is taken immediately <u>after</u> the birth or adoption. If you'd rather take some or all of your parental leave <u>before</u> the birth or adoption, you must inform your manager one month in advance.

1. Mrs. Lipa would rather _____.
2. Mrs. Lipa had better _____.

UNIT 8

Health and safety

Vocabulary

Objectives
- understand and give warnings
- explain consequences of carelessness
- make suggestions and agree to them

Picture dictionary

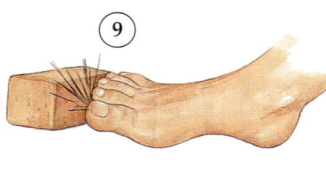
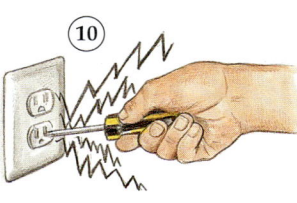

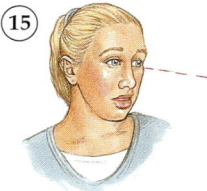
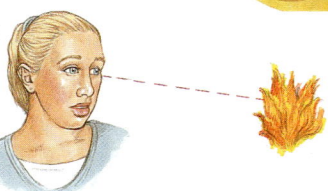

 A. Listen.

Safety and danger

1. a fire extinguisher
2. a smoke detector
3. a fire alarm
4. warning signs
5. slip
6. fall
7. jaywalk
8. get hit by a car
9. get hurt
10. get a shock
11. get burned
12. get sick
13. smell
14. hear
15. see

90 Unit 8

How often?

⑯ once a week   ⑰ twice a month   ⑱ three times a day

🎧 **B.** Listen again and repeat.

C. Answer the questions about <u>yourself</u>. Then compare your answers with a partner.

1. How many times a day do you drink water? _____
2. How many times a year do you go to the dentist? _____
3. How many times a week do you eat dinner at home? _____

🎧 **D.** Listen to the conversations. Then listen again and match each picture with a conversation. Write the letter on the line.

Conversation 1 _____   a.    b.    c.

Conversation 2 _____

Conversation 3 _____

▶ Do it yourself!

Look at the warning signs. Then complete the sentences with words from the box.

| get a shock | ~~get hit by a car~~ | get sick | get burned |

 1. Watch out! You might *get hit by a car* _____.

 2. Watch out! You might _____.

 3. Watch out! You might _____.

 4. Watch out! You might _____.

Practical conversations

Model 1   Warn someone about a danger.

A. Listen and read.

A: Watch out!
B: Why? What's wrong?
A: That's dangerous. You might get a shock.
B: You're right. Thanks for warning me.
A: You're welcome.

B. Listen again and repeat.

C. Pair work. Warn your partner. Use the warning signs.

get a shock   get burned   slip   get hurt

Warnings
Watch out!
Look out!
Be careful!

A: _____!
B: Why? What's wrong?
A: That's dangerous. You might _____.
B: You're right. Thanks for warning me.
A: _____.

Model 2   Report a dangerous situation and suggest action.

A. Listen and read.

A: Uh-oh. I hear water.
B: You'd better check the kitchen. I'll check the supply room.
A: Good idea. I'll be right back.
B: Me too.

B. Listen again and repeat.

C. Pair work. Express concern. Make a suggestion. Use the pictures and rooms from your home or workplace.

A: Uh-oh. I _____.
B: You'd better check the _____.
   I'll check the _____.
A: _____. I'll be right back.
B: Me too.

Model 3 Remind someone to do something.

A. Listen and read.

A: How often should I test the fire extinguisher?
B: Once a year. It's important. Don't forget.
A: I won't.
B: And remember to test the smoke detector too.
A: Don't worry. I will.

B. Listen again and repeat.

C. Pair work. Remind someone to do something. Use the words in the box and real times.

| the batteries | the fire alarm | the smoke detector | the fire extinguisher |

A: How often should I test _____?
B: _____ a _____. It's important. Don't forget.
A: I won't.
B: And remember to test _____ too.
A: _____. I will.

▶ Do it yourself!

Pair work. Look at the safety problems in the room. Create a conversation for the two people. Give warnings and suggest action.

Unit 8   93

Practical grammar

Might

Don't go near the stove. You **might** get burned.

A. Look at the pictures. Then complete the warnings. Use **might** and the words in the box.

| get sick | slip | get hit by a car | ~~get a shock~~ | get burned |

1.  Don't touch that! You _might get a shock_ .

2.  Don't jaywalk! You _____.

3.  Don't eat that! You _____.

4.  Don't put your hand on the engine! You _____ _____.

5.  Don't walk on that wet floor! You _____.

94   Unit 8

Responding with I will and I won't

B. Complete each conversation with I will or I won't.

1. **A:** Please tell me if you smell smoke.
   B: Don't worry. _____.

2. **A:** Don't touch that plug. You'll get a shock.
   B: _____.

3. **A:** Talk to your manager tomorrow.
   B: OK. _____.

4. **A:** If you get hurt, call the medical department.
   B: No problem. _____.

5. **A:** Please remember to check for gas.
   B: All right. _____.

6. **A:** Don't forget to replace the battery.
   B: _____.

▶ Do it yourself!

Pair work. Choose a warning sign. Tell your partner what might happen.

Unit 8   95

Authentic practice 1

With words you know, YOU can talk to this foreman.

A. Listen and read.

Foreman: There are a couple of important things I need to tell you. Mostly about safety. Why don't we meet in about ten minutes?

YOU *Excuse me?*

Foreman: Let's talk in about ten minutes.

YOU *OK. That's fine.*

[10 minutes later]

Foreman: OK. Two things here you've got to watch out for: fire and spills.

YOU *Fire? No problem. Where are the fire extinguishers?*

Foreman: To the left of all the exit doors. Remember that.

YOU *I will. But I don't understand—what are spills?*

Foreman: Spills? See this wet stuff on the floor? That's a spill. It's slippery. If you see a spill, be sure to put up a warning sign and call maintenance.

YOU *Well, thanks for warning me. I won't forget.*

B. Listen to the foreman. Read your part out loud.

C. Listen and read. Choose your response. Circle the letter.

1. "There are a couple of things I'd better tell you about."
   a. Sure. I'll be right back. **b.** It's important.

2. "Why don't we check the smoke detectors?"
   a. I don't know. **b.** Good idea.

3. "See that stuff over there? Don't touch it."
   a. I will. Thanks for warning me. **b.** I won't. Thanks for warning me.

D. Listen. Choose your response. Circle the letter.

1. a. I will. b. I won't.
2. a. What's wrong? b. Thanks for warning me.
3. a. Don't worry. I will. b. Don't worry. I won't.

Listening comprehension

A. Listen to the announcement. Then answer the questions. Circle the letter.

1. What is the speaker talking about?
   a. smoke detectors b. fire extinguishers
2. According to the speaker, what might save your life?
   a. smelling smoke b. hearing the beep-beep sound

B. Listen again. What should you remember about smoke detectors?

_____

C. In your own words. Answer the questions about smoke detectors and then discuss your answers with a partner.

1. Where are the smoke detectors where you live or work? _____
_____
2. Why are smoke detectors important? _____
_____

▶ Do it yourself!

A. Write your own response. Then read your conversation out loud with a partner.

Welcome. It's nice to have you at the plant.
YOU _____

Why don't we schedule some time to talk about safety?
YOU _____

But in the meantime, don't go near that stuff over there.
YOU _____

B. Personalization. Talk about fire extinguishers at home and at work. Where are they? Why are they important?

Authentic practice 2

Reading

A. Read the fire safety warnings.

B. Critical thinking. Read about these situations. Then choose advice for each person. Circle the letter.

Cueva

1. Julio Cueva is on the tenth floor, cooking dinner for his children. There's a small fire in his kitchen. He has a fire extinguisher. He knows how to use it.

   a. Use the fire extinguisher.   **b.** Take the elevator to the first floor and call 911.

   Explain your answer: *If the fire is small, use the fire extinguisher.*

Shufang

2. Li Shufang is working in a garage. There's a small fire in front of the exit door. She has a fire extinguisher, and she knows how to use it.

   a. Use the fire extinguisher.   **b.** Leave the building fast and call 911.

   Explain your answer: _____

Lulov

3. Marek Lulov discovers a small fire on the second floor at work. He has a fire extinguisher but isn't sure how to use it.

   a. Leave immediately. Go down the stairs. Call 911.   **b.** Call 911. Then use the fire extinguisher.

   Explain your answer: _____

Writing

A. On Saturday, Julio Cueva has a training session at work. His sister Paula is going to take care of his children. Read Julio's note to Paula.

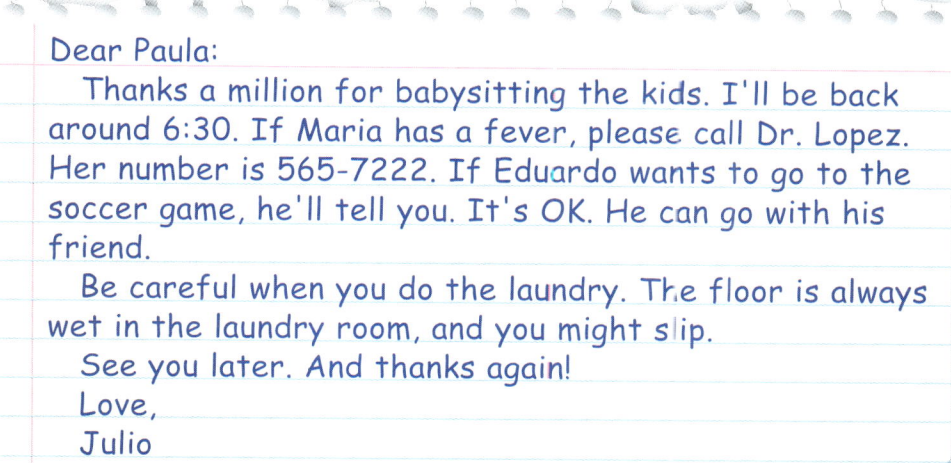

Dear Paula:
   Thanks a million for babysitting the kids. I'll be back around 6:30. If Maria has a fever, please call Dr. Lopez. Her number is 565-7222. If Eduardo wants to go to the soccer game, he'll tell you. It's OK. He can go with his friend.
   Be careful when you do the laundry. The floor is always wet in the laundry room, and you might slip.
   See you later. And thanks again!
   Love,
   Julio

B. Write a note to someone who is helping you with something. Thank the person and warn him or her about a possible problem. Use Julio's note as a model.

For extra practice, go to page 146.

➤ Do it yourself!   A plan-ahead project

Discussion. Find a fire extinguisher at home, at school, or at work. Read the directions. Or read the directions on this fire extinguisher. Talk about the directions with your classmates.

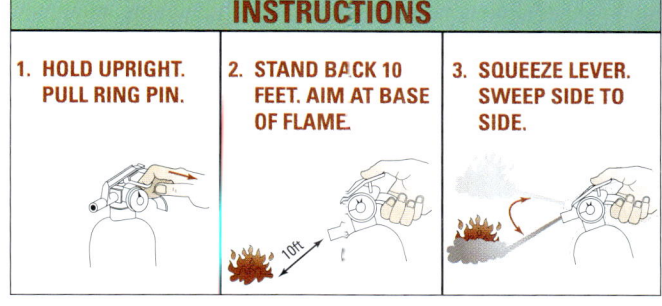

INSTRUCTIONS

1. HOLD UPRIGHT. PULL RING PIN.
2. STAND BACK 10 FEET. AIM AT BASE OF FLAME.
3. SQUEEZE LEVER. SWEEP SIDE TO SIDE.

Review

A. Vocabulary. Complete each sentence. Write the words on the line.

1. Don't touch that. You might _____.

fall / get burned

2. Don't jaywalk. You might _____.

get a shock / get hit by a car

3. Don't walk on that wet floor. You might _____.

get sick / slip

B. Conversation. Choose **your** response. Circle the letter.

1. "Don't forget. It's important."
   - **a.** I will.
   - **b.** I won't.

2. "Remember to check the smoke detector."
   - **a.** OK.
   - **b.** Me too.

3. "I'll be right back."
   - **a.** OK. See you soon.
   - **b.** Uh-oh.

4. "Why don't you check the hall?"
   - **a.** I don't know.
   - **b.** Good idea.

C. Grammar. Complete each response with **I will** or **I won't**.

1. "Remember to check the battery." OK, _____.
2. "Don't forget to install a smoke alarm on each floor." OK, _____.
3. "Please get a new fire extinguisher from the supply room." OK, _____.
4. "If you smell gas, call 911." OK, _____.

D. Reading and writing. Look at the signs. Write your **own** warning. Use **might**.

1. *Be careful. You might get sick.*

2. _____

3. _____

100   Unit 8

UNIT 9

Money

Objectives
- open a bank account
- fill out deposit and withdrawal slips
- read a bank statement
- record transactions in a check register

Vocabulary

Picture dictionary

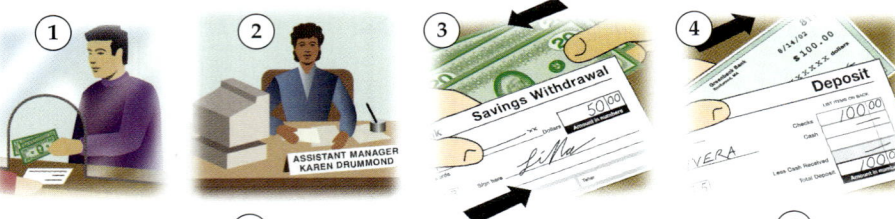

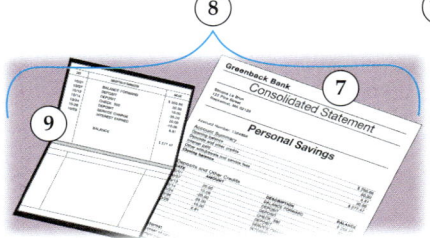

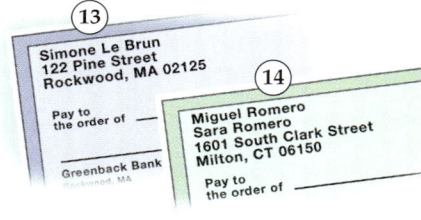

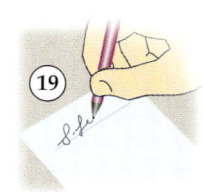
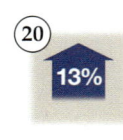

A. Listen.

Banking

1. a bank teller
2. a bank officer
3. a withdrawal
4. a deposit
5. a checking account
6. a checkbook
7. a statement
8. a savings account
9. a passbook
10. a check-cashing office
11. a certificate of deposit (a CD)
12. a holiday savings club
13. an individual account
14. a joint account
15. save
16. the front
17. the back
18. sign
19. endorse
20. high
21. low

102   Unit 9

Bank Statements

Account Summary	
Balance carried forward	$250.66
Monthly fee	$10.00 –
BALANCE	$240.66

Account Summary	
Balance carried forward	$300.53
Interest rate 3.5 %	
Interest earned	$10.52 +
BALANCE	$311.05

22) a fee

23) interest

B. Listen again and repeat.

C. Listen to the conversations. Then listen again and complete each sentence. Use words from the box.

> ATM fees   endorsing a check   a holiday savings club

Conversation 1 They're talking about _____.

Conversation 2 They're talking about _____.

Conversation 3 They're talking about _____.

D. Complete each sentence. Write the words on the line.

1. You can't deposit this check if you don't endorse the _____ and write your account number on it.
   front / back

2. I want a savings account with a _____ interest rate.
   high / low

3. I'd like a bank where the fees are _____.
   high / low

4. My husband and I would like to open _____ checking account.
   an individual / a joint

5. I think I was overcharged on my checking fees. Please look at my _____.
   statement / checkbook

➤ Do it yourself!

A. Personalization. Where do you save money? Where do your classmates save money? Complete the chart. Use these words or your own words.

> a savings account
> a holiday savings club
> a certificate of deposit (a CD)

Name	Where?
Alex	in a CD

Andre saves money in an IRA.

B. Collaborative activity. Where else do your classmates save money? Make a list and then discuss it.

Unit 9   103

Practical conversations

Model 1 Use a bank. Ask for information.

A. Listen and read.

A: I'd like to open a checking account.
B: Certainly. Just fill out this form and take it to an officer.
A: Oh. By the way, which CD pays the highest interest?
B: I'm not positive. I'll check.

B. Listen again and repeat.

C. Pair work. Use a bank. Ask for information. Use the ideas in the box.

make a deposit	deposit slip	a teller
make a withdrawal	withdrawal slip	a teller
apply for a credit card	form	an officer
open an account	form	an officer

A: I'd like to _____.
B: Certainly. Just fill out this _____ and take it to _____.
A: Oh. By the way, which _____ pays the highest interest?
B: I'm not positive. I'll check.

Model 2 Ask how long something will take.

A. Listen and read.

A: I'm interested in getting an ATM card.
B: OK. Why don't you have a seat? I'll get you the forms.
A: By the way, how long will it take?
B: It won't take long. About a week.

B. Listen again and repeat.

C. Pair work. Ask how long something will take. Use the ideas in the box.

A: I'm interested in _____.
B: _____. Why don't you have a seat? I'll get you the forms.
A: By the way, how long will it take?
B: It won't take long. About _____.

> opening a checking account
> applying for a credit card
> buying a CD

Model 3 Cash a check. Remember something you forgot to do.

A. Listen and read.

A: Excuse me. I'd like to cash this paycheck.
B: Sure. I'll be right with you.
A: Oops. I forgot to endorse the back. Just a second.
B: OK. How would you like that?
A: Let me think. . . . Twenties, tens, and singles, please.

B. Listen again and repeat.

C. Pair work. Cash a paycheck or a personal check. Remember something you forgot to do. Use the ideas in the box and your <u>own</u> words.

A: Excuse me. I'd like to cash this _____.
B: _____. I'll be right with you.
A: Oops. I forgot to _____. Just a _____.
B: _____. How would you like that?
A: Let me think. . . . _____, please.

> endorse the back
> fill out a deposit slip
> write my account number on the back

➤ Do it yourself!

A. Personalization. Complete the information on the paycheck and fill out the deposit slip. Use your <u>own</u> name and address.

B. Pair work. Create a conversation between a customer and a bank officer or teller. Use the check and deposit slip in your conversation.

"I'd like to deposit this check."

Unit 9

Practical grammar

Comparisons with adjectives: superlatives

Use comparatives to compare two people, places, or things.
Use superlatives to compare more than two people, places, or things.

adjective	comparative form	superlative form
high	higher	the highest
important	more important	the most important
good	better	the best
bad	worse	the worst

A. Complete each sentence with the superlative form of the adjective.

1. The check-cashing office on First Street is busier than the one on Main. But the one on Third Street is _the busiest_.
   _{busy}

2. The fees at National First Bank are lower than the fees at Green Bank. The fees at Key Credit Bank are _____.
   _{low}

3. You're getting 9% interest on a 3-month CD? That's _____ interest in the country.
   _{high}

4. What's _____ savings bank in the city?
   _{good}

5. What's _____ thing to ask about a holiday savings club?
   _{important}

6. I don't like to drive on the old road. It's _____ road in the state.
   _{dangerous}

7. This is _____ restaurant in town; it's dirty and the service is bad.
   _{bad}

Questions of degree

How **long** were you at the bank? For an hour.
How **soon** can you send me the checks? In about ten days.
How **high** is the interest rate on a passbook savings account? It's 3%, I think. But I'm not positive.

B. Complete each question with How and words from the box.

| ~~good~~ | busy | far | late | important | high | cold |

1. __How good__ is the customer service at the Mutual Bank?
2. _____ is the winter here?
3. _____ is the check-cashing office open?
4. _____ is a high interest rate when you choose a bank?
5. _____ are the ATM fees here?
6. _____ is the bank at lunch time?
7. _____ is your bank from your workplace?

▶ Do it yourself!

A. Personalization. What's your opinion? Fill out the survey about your city or town.

The best bank	
The best restaurant	
The best hospital	
The best clothing store	
The best supermarket	

B. Discussion. Compare opinions with your classmates.

Eduardo's has the best food.

Maybe. But how good is the service there?

Authentic practice 1

With words you know, YOU can talk to this bank officer.

🎧 **A.** Listen and read.

Officer: Good morning. What can we do for you today?
YOU I'd like to open an account.
Officer: Fine. What kind of account were you thinking of?
YOU A checking account.
Officer: Joint or individual?
YOU Joint, please. For me and my wife.
Officer: OK. Why don't you just step this way and have a seat? I'll be right with you.
YOU By the way, I'm interested in getting an ATM card too.
Officer: Certainly. I'll get you a form to fill out for your PIN.
YOU PIN?
Officer: Personal Identification Number. You'll need one for the ATM. Make yourself comfortable. I'll only be a minute.

🎧 **B.** Listen to the bank officer. Read **your** part out loud.

🎧 **C.** Listen and read. Choose **your** response. Circle the letter.

1. "What can we do for you today?"
   a. You can have a seat.
   b. I'm interested in opening an account.

2. "Please step this way. I'll be right with you."
   a. OK. Thank you.
   b. I'm not positive.

3. "Why don't you have a seat?"
   a. Thanks. I will.
   b. Because I already have one.

🎧 **D.** Listen. Choose **your** response. Circle the letter.

1. a. Joint or individual?   b. Oops, I forgot to endorse it. Just a second.
2. a. OK. Thanks.   b. Yes, please.
3. a. Fives and tens, thanks.   b. It won't take long.

Listening comprehension

A. Listen to the automated customer service line from the State Bank. Then read the Customer Services chart.

Customer Services

- ☐ Verify account balances
- ☐ Open a checking account
- ☐ Transfer money into another account
- ☐ Pay bills
- ☐ Talk to a financial adviser
- ☐ Open a savings account
- ☐ Apply for an ATM card
- ☐ Change a PIN number

B. Listen again. Check ☑ the <u>four</u> things you can do by telephone.

C. Listen again. Then answer the questions <u>yes</u>, <u>no</u>, or <u>I don't know</u>.

1. Does the caller have an account with the State Bank? _____
2. How many languages does the caller speak? _____

D. In your own words. Discuss these bank services: ATMs, automated customer service lines, talking to bank officers and tellers.
Which is the best? Which is the easiest? Which is the worst?

ATMs are the easiest.

▶ Do it yourself!

A. Write your <u>own</u> response. Then read your conversation out loud with a partner.

- Good afternoon. What can we do for you?
  YOU _____

- Certainly. Please have a seat at my desk.
  YOU _____

- I'll be right with you. I just have to get some forms.
  YOU _____

B. Personalization. In your opinion, what's a good bank? What's a bad bank?

Unit 9 109

Authentic practice 2

Reading

A. Look at the bank statement. Then check ✓ the information the statement has.

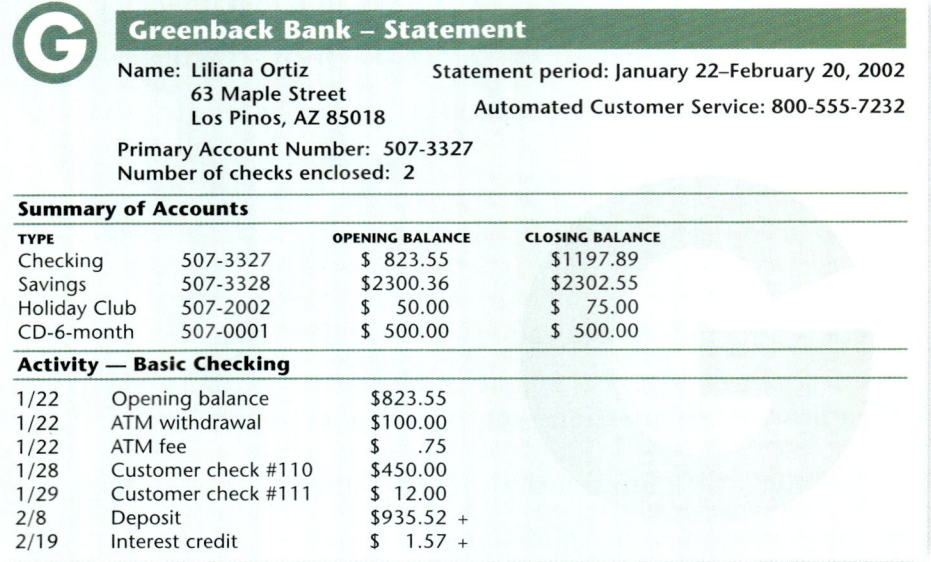

1. ☐ the customer's name
2. ☐ the customer's phone number
3. ☐ the interest rate for the 6-month CD
4. ☐ the statement period
5. ☐ the balance in the checking account
6. ☐ the bank's address
7. ☐ the customer service phone number
8. ☐ the deposits and withdrawals

B. Critical thinking. Look at these bank documents and the bank statement in Exercise A. Then answer the questions.

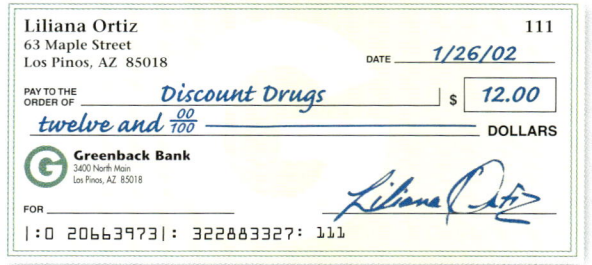

1. When did Ms. Ortiz make a deposit? _____
2. When did she get cash from the ATM? _____
3. When did she write the check to Marian Pappas? _____
4. How long did it take for the bank to receive the check Ms. Ortiz wrote to Discount Drugs? _____

Writing

A. Look at the entries in Liliana Ortiz's check register. Then answer the questions.

Ortiz

ITEM NO. OR TRANS. CODE	DATE	TRANSACTION DESCRIPTION	SUBTRACTIONS AMOUNT OF PAYMENT OR WITHDRAWAL (-)	(-) FEE IF ANY	ADDITIONS AMOUNT OF DEPOSIT OR PAYMENT (+)	BALANCE 823 55
	1/22	ATM withdrawal	100 00	.75		100 75
						722 80
110	1/24	Marian Pappas rent	450 00			450 00
						272 80
111	1/26	Discount Drugs	12 00			12 00
						260 80
	2/8	Deposit			935 52	935 52
						1196 32
	2/19	Interest			1 57	1 57
						1197 89

1. How much money did Ms. Ortiz withdraw from the ATM? _____
2. What was the fee? _____

B. Enter the transactions for the activity on February 22, 23, and 25. Use the check register in Exercise A.

```
DATE              TIME           LOCATION
Feb 22, 2002      8:14           002249

TRANSACTION       AMOUNT         DESCRIPTION
GOT CASH          $80.00         FROM CHECKING
ATM FEE           $ .75
```

Greenback Bank
3400 North Main
Los Pinos, AZ 85018

DEPOSIT TICKET

Liliana Ortiz
63 Maple Street
Los Pinos, AZ 85018

CASH ▶
CHECKS ▶ 800 00

DATE 2/23/02   TOTAL $ 800.00
322883327: 28

Liliana Ortiz   112
63 Maple Street
Los Pinos, AZ 85018   DATE 2/25/02

PAY TO THE
ORDER OF Dr. Stanley Arzoomanian $ 45.00

Forty-five ——————————— DOLLARS

Greenback Bank
3400 North Main
Los Pinos, AZ 85018

FOR _____   Liliana Ortiz
|:0 20663973|: 322883327: 112

For extra practice, go to page 147.

➤ Do it yourself!   A plan-ahead project

Discussion. Collect bank documents such as withdrawal slips, deposit slips, and deposit envelopes from your bank. Then compare them with the ones your classmates found.

- How are they the same?
- How are they different?
- Which ones are the easiest to use?

Review

A. Vocabulary. Complete each sentence. Write the words on the line.

1. What's the interest rate on a one-year _____?
   _{passbook / CD}

2. I'm leaving the Greenback Savings Bank. The fees are too _____.
   _{high / low}

3. You'd better _____ the back of the check if you want to deposit it.
   _{endorse / save}

B. Conversation. Choose <u>your</u> response. Circle the letter.

1. "How would you like that?"
   a. In fives and tens.
   b. I'd like to cash this check.

2. "Just a minute. I'll be right with you."
   a. Great.
   b. You're right.

3. "I'll check."
   a. Where do I endorse it?
   b. Thanks. How long will it take?

C. Grammar. Complete each sentence. Write an adjective on the line.

1. How _____ are the fees at Mid-State Bank?
   _{high / higher}

2. Which bank has the _____ customer service in town?
   _{better / best}

3. How _____ is good service?
   _{important / most important}

4. That check-cashing office has the _____ check-cashing fees in this city.
   _{worse / worst}

D. Reading and writing. Look at the check and the deposit slip. Record the transactions in the check register.

ITEM NO. OR TRANS. CODE	DATE	TRANSACTION DESCRIPTION	SUBTRACTIONS AMOUNT OF PAYMENT OR WITHDRAWAL (-)	(-) FEE IF ANY	ADDITIONS AMOUNT OF DEPOSIT OR PAYMENT(+)	BALANCE
						457 22

112 Unit 9

UNIT 10

Your career

Vocabulary

Objectives
- understand company-paid benefits
- follow company policies
- understand paychecks and pay stubs

Picture dictionary

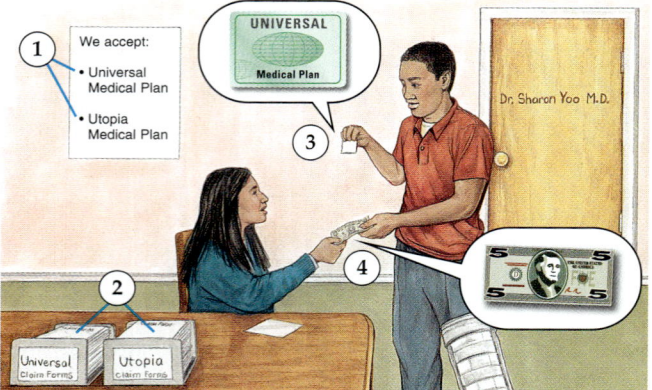

A. Listen.

Health insurance
1. a medical plan
2. claim forms
3. an insurance card
4. a co-payment
5. a dental plan
6. a vision plan
7. a reimbursement
8. sign up
9. a dependent
10. choose

Benefits and related words
11. a vacation
12. retirement
13. a pension
14. a salary

114   Unit 10

Employment

⑮ **employed**: has a job

⑯ **unemployed**: doesn't have a job

⑰ **self-employed**: doesn't have a boss

🎧 **B.** Listen again and repeat.

🎧 **C.** Listen to the conversations. Then listen again and complete each sentence. Use words from the box.

| a dental plan | a reimbursement | a pension |

Conversation 1 They're talking about _____.

Conversation 2 They're talking about _____.

Conversation 3 They're talking about _____.

D. Complete each sentence. Write the words on the line.

Mr. and Mrs. Diaz live in Miami. Mr. Diaz works at King's Dental Supply, and Mrs. Diaz is _____. She has her own business—she sells clothes
_{1. unemployed / self-employed}

from Santo Domingo. Their son Joe is _____ right now. He's looking
_{2. unemployed / self-employed}

for a job.

King's Dental Supply has great _____ for employees and
_{3. health insurance / co-payments}

their _____, so Mrs. Diaz and Joe are covered too. For the
_{4. dependents / reimbursements}

_____ plan, all they have to do is _____ a doctor
_{5. medical / dental}   _{6. choose / sign up}

and pay a small _____ when they have an appointment.
_{7. co-payment / reimbursement}

▶ Do it yourself!

A. What kinds of benefits do you and your classmates have? Complete the chart with numbers.

B. Discussion. Talk about other kinds of benefits you or your classmates have.

Benefit	Number of students who have this benefit
a medical plan	
a dental plan	
a vision plan	
a retirement pension	
other benefits	

Practical conversations

Model 1   Ask about a benefits plan. Remind someone about an obligation.

A. Listen and read.

A: Have you signed up for the medical plan yet?
B: Yes, I have.
A: And have you chosen a doctor?
B: No, I haven't. Not yet.
A: Well, we're supposed to do that by 5:00 today.
B: I know. Thanks for reminding me.

B. Listen again and repeat.

C. Pair work. Ask about a benefits plan. Remind your partner about an obligation. Use the words in the box.

| medical plan | a doctor | dental plan | a dentist | vision plan | an optician |

A: Have you signed up for the _____ yet?
B: Yes, I have.
A: And have you chosen _____?
B: No, I haven't. Not yet.
A: Well, we're supposed to do that by _____.
B: I know. Thanks for reminding me.

Model 2   Break news. Express surprise and approval.

A. Listen and read.

A: Hey, Monica, guess what!
B: What?
A: We're going to get six more vacation days.
B: No kidding. That's terrific. When does the new policy start?
A: Immediately.

B. Listen again and repeat.

Approval
terrific
wonderful
fantastic

C. Pair work. Break news about a vacation or sick day policy. Use the words in the box and your own words.

A: Hey, _____, guess what!
B: What?
A: We're going to get _____.
B: No kidding. That's _____. When does the new policy start?
A: _____.

> four more sick days
> five more vacation days

Model 3   Meet an old friend. Discuss bad news. Make a suggestion.

A. Listen and read.

A: Hi, Jack. Long time, no see. How's it going?
B: Not great. I lost my job.
A: Oh, no. How long have you been unemployed?
B: Since March 13.
A: Why don't you ask about a job where I work? There are some openings right now. And we have very good benefits.

B. Listen again and repeat.

Periods of time
Since March 13
Since last year / yesterday / Tuesday
For six weeks

C. Pair work. Talk about losing a job. Make suggestions. Use the benefits in the box and your own words.

> vision plan   dental plan   sick leave policy
> medical plan   vacation policy

A: Hi, _____. Long time, no see. How's it going?
B: _____. I lost my job.
A: Oh, no. How long have you been unemployed?
B: _____.
A: Why don't you ask about a job where I work? There are some openings right now. And we have a terrific _____.

▶ Do it yourself!

Pair work. Create a conversation for the people in the picture. Talk about benefits plans.

Practical grammar

The present perfect with already and yet, for and since

Use have or has and a past participle for the present perfect. The past participle of regular verbs is like the simple past form (verb + -ed).

I **have worked** here for a year. Maria **has lived** in Chicago since May.

Past participles of irregular verbs

Verb	Past participle		Verb	Past participle
be	been		read	read
choose	chosen		speak	spoken
do	done		take	taken

There is a complete list of past participles of irregular verbs on page 135.

A. Complete the present perfect form of each verb.

1. Have you _____taken_____ all your sick days yet? (take)
2. How long has he _____ in that plan? (be)
3. They have already _____ to their doctor about the co-payment. (speak)
4. Haven't you _____ the claim form yet? (read)
5. We've already _____ the plan, but it hasn't started yet. (choose)
6. I haven't _____ that since last year. (do)
7. We _____ at Rosa's Painting for five years. (work)
8. How long _____ they _____ employed here? (be)
9. She _____ her vacation days since 2001. (not take)

Be supposed to and suggestions with Why

Are we supposed to sign up today?

Don't forget to sign up for the new medical plan.

Hi Louise. When are we supposed to sign up?

I'm not sure. Why don't we call Louise in Benefits?

You were supposed to do that yesterday. But it's not too late. Why don't you come to my office and pick up the forms?

B. Complete the conversations. Use the present or past of be supposed to or make a suggestion with Why.

1. A: _____ your insurance card? You'll need it if your name
    Why / you / bring
    isn't in the computer.
   B: OK. And _____ the co-payment at the time of the doctor visit?
    we / pay

2. A: _____ a doctor before we signed up?
    we / choose
   B: I think so. _____ the policy again?
    Why / we / read

3. A: _____ to a dentist who's not on the list. The plan won't pay.
    You / not / go
   B: That's right. _____ the new list?
    Why / we / get

4. A: I'm not sure when we have to choose a new doctor. _____ in
    Benefits?   *Why / we / check*
   B: Good idea. I think _____ next week.
    we / choose

➤ Do it yourself!

A. Read the problems. Write suggestions with Why don't you or Why don't we.

1. I'm supposed to sign up, but I don't have the enrollment form.

   1. Why don't you get one from Benefits?

2. I saw the optician two months ago, but I haven't received the reimbursement yet.

   2. _____

3. I don't know what we're supposed to do when we take a sick day.

   3. _____

B. Pair work. Read your conversations out loud with a partner.

Authentic practice 1

> With words you know, YOU can talk to this former co-worker.

A. Listen and read.

Eva: Hey, Elaine! I haven't seen you in ages. How're you doing?
YOU: *Eva! I'm OK! What about you?*
Eva: Well, to tell you the truth, pretty bad. I lost my job.
YOU: *Oh, no. You lost your job? I'm sorry.*
Eva: Yeah, well, they closed the office and everyone got laid off.
YOU: *That's awful.*
Eva: Well, I still have my benefits. And I'm getting unemployment. But I'm looking for a new job.
YOU: *Why don't you talk to Ann in Customer Service? There are some openings right now.*
Eva: Really?
YOU: *Yeah. I'll call Ann tomorrow morning. She really liked you. You were a great cashier.*
Eva: Thanks a million. I'm supposed to go to the unemployment office at 9:00, and I'd better be on time. What if I come in at about 10:00?
YOU: *That's great. See you then.*

B. Listen to Eva. Read your part out loud.

C. Listen and read. Choose your response. Circle the letter.

1. "I haven't seen you in ages."
   a. I know. Long time, no see.
   b. That's good. What about you?

2. "To tell you the truth, our benefits are terrible."
   a. No kidding. That's too bad.
   b. That's terrific.

3. "What if I call Ann?"
   a. That sounds fine.
   b. Why don't you call Ann?

🎧 **D. Listen. Choose your response. Circle the letter.**

1. a. Not great. b. I'm going to sign up.
2. a. How long have you been unemployed? b. Really? I'm sorry!
3. a. Yes! Thanks for reminding me. b. Guess what!

Listening comprehension

🎧 **A. Listen to the conversation. Then listen again and check ☑ old plan or new plan.**

	old plan	new plan
1. Employees can use this year's vacation days next year.	☐	☐
2. Employees can't use this year's vacation days next year.	☐	☐
3. Employees get four weeks of vacation after seven years.	☐	☐
4. Employees get four weeks of vacation after five years.	☐	☐
5. Employees have three sick days.	☐	☐
6. Employees have five sick days.	☐	☐

B. In your own words. Answer the questions. Then discuss your answers with a partner.

1. What do you think is a good vacation or sick day policy? _____

2. Who takes more vacation and sick days—people who work for a company, or people who are self-employed? _____

▶ Do it yourself!

A. Write your own response. Then read your conversation out loud with a partner.

It's been ages since I've seen you. How's it going?
YOU _____

Really?
YOU _____

What if I call you tomorrow?
YOU _____

B. Personalization. Talk about how many vacation days and sick days you've used this year.

Authentic practice 2

Reading

A. Read Katrin Havel's paycheck and pay stub. Then complete each sentence. Circle the letter.

Paycheck:
Edison Lighting
Mutual Bank
Crane, Washington 98343
Date: 06/15/02
Check No: 2330051
PAY FIVE HUNDRED NINETY AND 39/100 .... DOLLARS
$*****590.39
TO THE ORDER OF Katrin Havel

Havel

Pay stub:
Edison Lighting
DATE: 06/15/02
CHECK NO: 2330051
KATRIN HAVEL   PAY PERIOD: 6/01/02 TO 6/15/02

HOURS AND EARNINGS		TAXES AND DEDUCTIONS	
GROSS PAY	$737.10	MEDICAL INSURANCE	$8.55
		DENTAL INSURANCE	$2.66
		FEDERAL TAX	$85.20
		STATE TAX	$50.30
NET PAY	$590.39	TOTAL DEDUCTIONS	$146.71

RATE $10.53
HOURS   70.00
EARNINGS $737.10   YEAR-TO-DATE $8104.80

PRE-TAX ITEMS   AFTER-TAX DEDUCTIONS

1. Ms. Havel works at _____.
   a. Mutual Bank   b. Edison Lighting

2. June 1 to June 15 is a _____.
   a. paycheck   b. pay period

3. Each month Ms. Havel gets money — her _____.
   a. earnings   b. deductions

4. Each month Ms. Havel pays money — her _____.
   a. deductions   b. earnings

5. The money she gets <u>before</u> the deductions are taken out is her _____ pay.
   a. gross   b. net

6. The money she gets <u>after</u> the deductions are taken out is her _____ pay.
   a. gross   b. net

B. Critical thinking. Read the pay stub again. Then answer the questions.

1. How much money has Ms. Havel earned this year? _____
2. How much has she earned this month? _____
3. Which benefit plans has she enrolled in? _____

122   Unit 10

4. How much federal tax did Ms. Havel pay in this pay period? _____

5. How much state tax did she pay in this pay period? _____

6. How many hours did Ms. Havel work in this pay period? _____

Writing

A. Katrin Havel's new husband is a self-employed electrician. He's uninsured, so Ms. Havel enrolls her husband in her medical plan. Read the form. Then answer the questions.

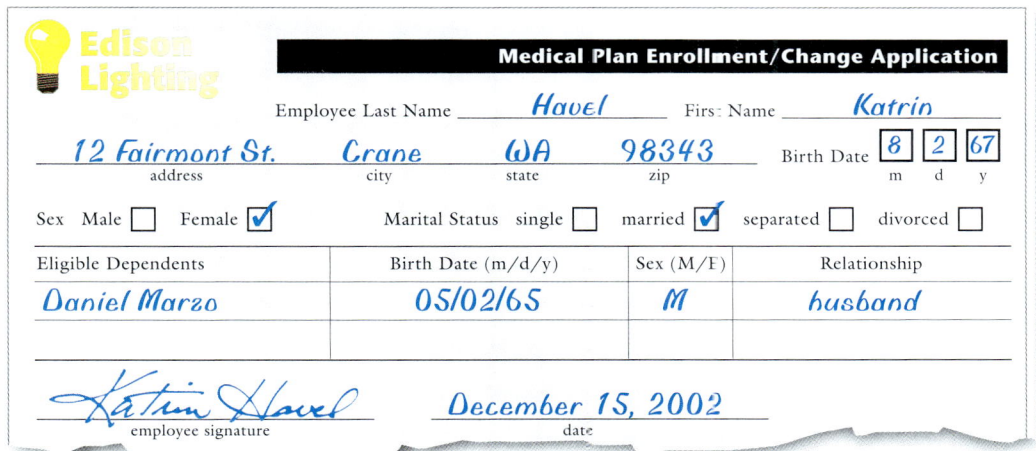

1. How many dependents does Ms. Havel have? _____
2. When did she enroll her husband in the plan? _____

B. Enroll your <u>own</u> dependent in the medical plan.

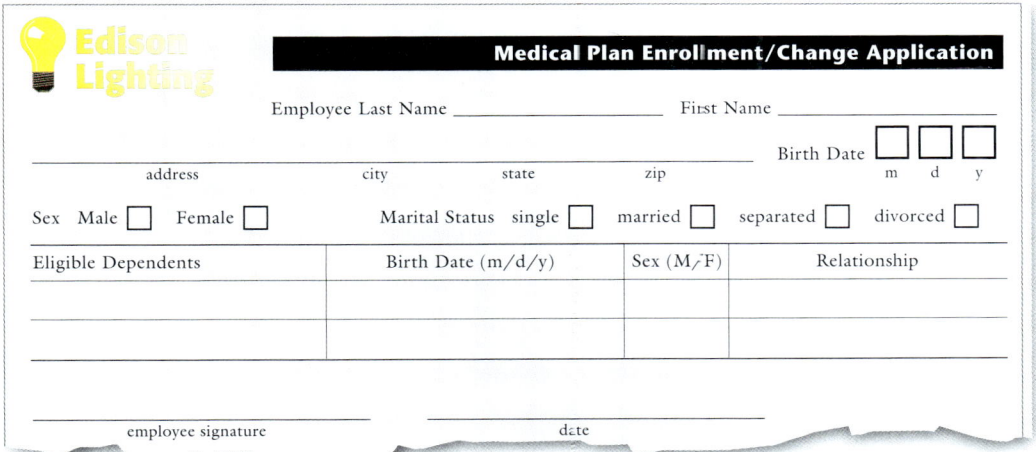

For extra practice, go to page 148.

▶ Do it yourself!

Discussion. Talk about your own benefits plan, or talk about a friend's or a family member's benefits. Compare benefits with your classmates. Discuss vacation policies, medical and dental plans, and retirement benefits.

Review

A. Vocabulary. Complete each sentence. Write the words on the line.

The _____ at this company are terrific! There's a long list of
      1. co-payments / benefits

doctors for the _____ plan, and when you visit the doctor, you only
           2. medical / retirement

have to pay a small _____. You can retire at age 55 with a good
              3. salary / co-payment

_____ and medical benefits for yourself and your _____.
  4. salary / pension   5. dependents / benefits

B. Conversation. Choose **your** response. Circle the letter.

1. "How long have you been self-employed?"
   a. No kidding.
   b. Since early last year.

2. "Guess what!"
   a. What?
   b. Thanks for reminding me.

3. "Long time, no see."
   a. Why don't you get a vision plan?
   b. Hi! How's it going?

C. Grammar. Complete each sentence with the present perfect.

1. They _have been_ in this country since 2000.
            be
2. Karl _____ here for two years.
              work
3. She _____ a vacation yet this year.
            not take
4. Marie _____ already _____ her doctor.
                                              choose
5. _____ you already _____ to Benefits about that?
                                          speak

D. Reading and writing. Find the mistake. What is the the correct net pay? _____

	FLORENCIA BAKER		CHECK NO: FW31111	
	EARNINGS		**DEDUCTIONS**	
	GROSS PAY	$800.50	MEDICAL INSURANCE	$6.30
			DENTAL INSURANCE	$2.40
			FICA	$40.66
			FEDERAL TAX	$90.35
Fabric World, Inc.			STATE TAX	$55.20
	NET PAY	$665.59	TOTAL DEDUCTIONS	$194.91

124   Unit 10

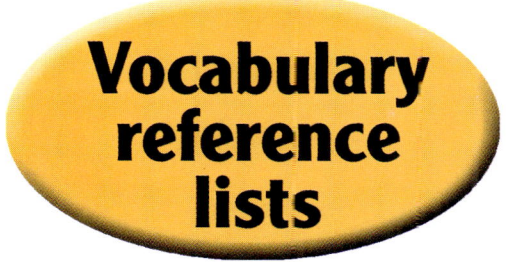

Vocabulary reference lists

Alphabetical word list

This is an alphabetical list of all active vocabulary in *Ready to Go 2*. The numbers refer to the page on which the word first appears. When a word has two meanings (a new brush OR Brush your hair), both are in the list.

A
a   70
account   104
account number   103
across the street   19
actions   30
after   54
afternoon   6
against the rules   80
agree   79
already   57
an   70
answer (the phone)   8
apartment   18
apply   104
appreciate   68
around the corner   19
arrive   54
assistant   2
ATM   103
ATM card   104
awful   7

B
back   102
bad   7
bank   102
bank officer   102
bank teller   102
banking   102
basement   18
bath mat   66
bathroom   18
bathtub   66
batteries   93
be stuck in traffic   54
beautiful   7
bed   66
bedroom   18
before   54
benefits   114
better   46
blanket   66
boss   79
brake pedal   30
brand   42
break the rules   78

breakfast   6
brother-in-law   79
brush *n.*   42
brush *v.*   43
bucket   66
bus   54
bus stop   18
buy   54

C
camera   42
car   30
carefully   21
carpet   67
cart   68
cash   105
certificate of deposit
   [a CD]   102
change   67
change the sheets   67
cheap   44
check *n.*   105
check *v.*   30
check-cashing office   102
checkbook   102
checking account   102
child, children   78
chilly   5
choose   114
claim form   114
clean   42
cleansers   66
close   32
cloudy   6
co-payment   114
co-worker   78
coat   6
cold   6
comb *n.*   42
comb *v.*   43
community   78
commuting   54
convenience store   18
cool   6
cough medicine   42
could   58
cover   115
credit card   104

D
danger   90
dangerous   92
daughter-in-law   78
day shift   80
dental plan   114
dentist   116
deodorant   42
dependent   114
deposit   102
deposit slip   104
desk   66
dinner   6
dirty   42
disagree   78
discuss   78
discuss a problem   78
do   67
do the laundry   67
doctor   116
door   30
down the street   19
drive   33
drop off   31
drugstore   42

E
early shift   80
either   70
electric bill   18
elevator   18
employed   115
employee   78
employer   78
empty   67
empty the trash   67
endorse   102
engine   30
estimate   32
express   54

F
fall   90
family   78
fare   54
fare card   54
father-in-law   78

129

favor   68
fee   103
few   20
fill out   104
fill up   31
film   42
fire alarm   90
fire extinguisher   90
first shift   80
flat tire   54
for   118
forget   105
form   104
front   102
full-time   80
funny sound   32
furniture polish   66

G

gas   30
gas bill   18
gas pedal   30
get a promotion   78
get a shock   90
get along   78
get burned   90
get fired   78
get hired   78
get hit by a car   90
get hurt   90
get sick   90
give   21
glad   68
glass cleaner   66
go off   32
go on   32
good   7
grandparent   78
great   7
ground floor   18

H

had better   83
hair dryer   42
headlight   30
health insurance   114
hear   90
help   68
her   10
high   102
him   10
holiday savings club   102
hood   30
horn   33

horrible   7
hot   6
house   18
housework   67
housing   18
how high   107
how long   107
how soon   107
hurry   57

I

if   82
immediately   116
in-law   79
individual account   102
information   104
inside   6
insurance card   114
interest   103
interest rate   103
it   22

J

jaywalk   90
joint account   102

K

kitchen   18

L

landlord   78
late shift   80
laundry   67
laundry room   18
lease   21
leave   54
leave a message   8
living room   18
local   54
look for   20
low   102
lunch   6

M

make   67
make a deposit   104
make a withdrawal   104
make the bed   67
manager   79
me   10
meal   6
medical plan   114
medicine   42
message   8

might   94
miss   54
miss the bus   54
money   81
mop   66
morning   6
mother-in-law   79

N

nearby   20
neighbor   78
neighborhood   18
new   30
next   56
next door   19
nice   20
night   6
night shift   80

O

offer   68
oil   30
oil pressure   33
on sale   44
one way   54
one-way ticket   55
only   44
open   32
open an account   104
opening   116
optician   116
outside   6
overcharge   45
owner   80

P

painkillers   42
paper towels   66
parent   78
park   18
part-time   80
partner   78
parts department   2
passbook   102
paycheck   105
pension   114
personal call   80
personal care product   42
photocopier   5
pick up   31
pickup truck   30
pillow   66
pillowcase   66
policy   116

price 42
problem 32
product 30
put away 68

Q
question 20

R
radio 33
rain check 44
raincoat 6
raining 6
reimbursement 114
relating 78
relationship 78
relative 78
remove 30
rent 20
repair 32
repeat 4
replace 30
retirement 114
ring up 45
round trip 54
rubber gloves 66
rules 80
run out of 54

S
safety 90
salary 114
sale price 42
save 102
savings account 102
seat 104
second floor 18
second shift 80
security deposit 21
see 90
self-employed 115
shampoo 42
sheet 66
should 58
show 20
shower 66
sick day 117
sign 21
sign up 114
since 118
sink 66
sister-in-law 79
slip 90
smell 90

smoke detector 90
snowing 6
soap 42
sold out 44
son-in-law 79
soon 57
speak 5
special 45
sponge 66
start 32
statement 102
store brand 44
store owner 78
stove 94
subway station 18
sunny 6
supervisor 79
supplies 69
supply closet 66
supply room 69
SUV 30

T
take a bus 54
take a message 8
take a picture 43
take a taxi 54
take a train 54
taxi 54
teeth 43
teller 104
terrible 7
terrific 7
the 70
them 22
thermometer 42
ticket 54
time of day 6
tire 30
tissues 42
today 20
toilet 66
toilet paper 66
token 54
tomorrow 20
tonight 20
too 70
toothbrush 42
toothpaste 42
tow truck 30
towel 66
traffic 54
train 54
transportation 54
trash 67

trash bags 66
truck 30
trunk 30
turn off 31
turn on 31
turn signal 33
TV 33

U
umbrella 6
unemployed 115
us 10
use 54
used *adj.* 30
usually 44

V
vacation 114
vacation day 116
vacuum 67
vacuum cleaner 66
van 30
VCR 33
vision plan 114

W
warm 6
warn 92
warning 92
warning light 33
warning sign 90
wash 43
washcloth 66
weather 6
which 47
will / won't 10
window 30
windshield wipers 30
withdrawal 102
withdrawal slip 104
wonderful 116
work *n.* 33
work *v.* 80
work it out 81
working 32
worse 46
would 11
would rather 83

Y
yet 56
you 10

Key expressions

This is a unit-by-unit list of all the social language from the practical conversations in *Ready to Go 2*.

Welcome to *Ready to Go*

Hi.
How's it going?
Great.
What about you?
Fine, thanks.
Mary, this is John. John, this is Mary.
Nice to meet you.
Nice to meet you too.
Where are you from?
Me? (for clarification)
And you?
What do you do?
I work in the _____ department.
Well, I have to go now.
Nice meeting you.
See you later.
Excuse me. (to start a conversation)
I'm looking for Mr. Yu.
Mr. Yu? (for clarification)
How do you spell that?
Just a minute.
Oh, yes.
I'm sorry. (to introduce a request)
Could you repeat that, please?
Sure. (to agree to a request)
Thanks.
You're welcome.

Unit 1

Can I help you?
Yes, please.
This is _____. (telephone identification)
I'm calling _____.
Is he in?
Just a moment, please.
It's for you. (to give someone the telephone)
Hello. (telephone greeting)
Is _____ there?
No, I'm sorry. (to express regret)
He's not in right now.
Who's calling?
When will he be back?
I'm not sure.
Would you like to leave a message?
My number's _____.
Oh, hi.
What's it like outside?
By the way, (to introduce a new topic)
Are there any messages for me?

Unit 2

I'm looking for _____.
Well, _____. (to introduce a thought)
How much is _____? (to ask for the cost or price)
$550 a month.
I have a few questions about _____.
Sure. (to respond to a statement or question)
Right around the corner.
What about _____? (to introduce an additional question)
OK. (to agree)
Is there anything else?
It's one month's rent.
That's fine.
No problem.

Unit 3

You can pick it up at about five.
Can you give me an estimate?
It'll be about $50.00. (to give an estimate)
_____ speaking. (to answer the phone)
My _____ aren't working.
What kind of car is it?
That's good for me. (to agree to a suggestion)
I'm here to drop off my car.
What's the problem?
Great! (to respond enthusiastically)
I'll give you a call.

Unit 4

How much is the one over here? (to ask for a price)
Do you have any _____? (to ask for an item in a store)
They're on sale.
They're only $9.99.
That'll be $7.21, please.
This _____ 's on sale for $_____.
I'm sorry, but _____. (to express / introduce an opposing idea / thought / opinion)
That price is for the store brand.
We're sold out.
That's too bad. (to express disappointment)
Will you give me a rain check?
Here you go.
It's good for a month.
I think I was overcharged.
Oh, I'm sorry. (to express regret; to apologize)
Let me have a look.
See, _____. (to show proof)
I'll ring it up again.

Unit 5

One ticket to _____, please.
Round trip or one way?
What's the fare?
When's the next train?
In ten minutes.
At 8:15.
You just missed it.
It left five minutes ago.
Oh, no. (to express disappointment)
They leave every 15 minutes.
Can I still make the 5:22?

Unit 6

Could you please _____? (to ask for a favor)
I'd be glad to.
Anything else?
Thanks for the help.
Anytime (to respond to a thank-you)
Would you like me to _____? (to offer help)
Thanks for offering, but I can do that myself.
Please let me know if there's anything I can do.
Actually, you could _____. (to accept an offer of help)
I do too.
I'll be right back.
Thanks a million.

Unit 7

I have a question.
What will happen if I make a personal call?
It's against the rules.
You'd better not.
Really? (to express surprise)
Well, thanks for telling me.
That's a good question.
I'd better check with my wife.
Tomorrow's fine.
I just don't get along with my in-laws.
I'm sorry to hear that. (to express sympathy)
You can work it out.
I guess it's worth a try.

Unit 8

Watch out!
What's wrong?
You're right.
Uh-oh.
Good idea.
Me too.
How often should I _____?
Don't forget.
Remember to _____.
Don't worry.
I will.
I won't.

Unit 9

Certainly.
I'm not positive.
I'll check.
I'm interested in getting an ATM card.
Why don't you have a seat?
I'll get you the forms.
How long will it take?
It won't take long.
About a week.
I'll be right with you.
Oops. (to remember something you forgot to do)
Just a second.
How would you like that? (to ask about monetary denomination)
Let me think....
Twenties, tens, and singles, please.

Unit 10

Yes, I have.
No, I haven't.
Not yet.
We're supposed to do that by 5:00 today.
I know.
Guess what?
What? (as a response to a question)
No kidding. (to show disbelief)
That's terrific.
Immediately.
Long time, no see.
Not great.
I lost my job.
Since March 13.

Irregular verbs

The following verbs from *Ready to Go 2* have irregular past-tense forms.

Base form	Past-tense form	Past participle
be	was / were	been
break	broke	broken
bring	brought	brought
buy	bought	bought
choose	chose	chosen
come	came	come
do	did	done
drink	drank	drunk
drive	drove	driven
eat	ate	eaten
fall	fell	fallen
fight	fought	fought
find	found	found
forget	forgot	forgotten
get	got	gotten
give	gave	given
go	went	gone
have	had	had
hear	heard	heard
hit	hit	hit
hurt	hurt	hurt
know	knew	known
leave	left	left
let	let	let
lose	lost	lost
make	made	made
mean	meant	meant
meet	met	met
pay	paid	paid
put	put	put
read	read	read
ring	rang	rung
run	ran	run
say	said	said
see	saw	seen
sell	sold	sold
send	sent	sent
speak	spoke	spoken
take	took	taken
tell	told	told
think	thought	thought
understand	understood	understood
wear	wore	worn
withdraw	withdrew	withdrawn
write	wrote	written

U.S. postal abbreviations

State/Possession	Abbreviation	State/Possession	Abbreviation
Alabama	AL	Pennsylvania	PA
Alaska	AK	Puerto Rico	PR
American Samoa	AS	Rhode Island	RI
Arizona	AZ	South Carolina	SC
Arkansas	AR	South Dakota	SD
California	CA	Tennessee	TN
Colorado	CO	Texas	TX
Connecticut	CT	Utah	UT
Delaware	DE	Vermont	VT
District of Columbia	DC	Virgin Islands	VI
Federated States of Micronesia	FM	Virginia	VA
Florida	FL	Washington	WA
Georgia	GA	West Virginia	WV
Guam	GU	Wisconsin	WI
Hawaii	HI	Wyoming	WY
Idaho	ID		
Illinois	IL		
Indiana	IN		
Iowa	IA		
Kansas	KS		
Kentucky	KY		
Louisiana	LA		
Maine	ME		
Marshall Islands	MH		
Maryland	MD		
Massachusetts	MA		
Michigan	MI		
Minnesota	MN		
Mississippi	MS		
Missouri	MO		
Montana	MT		
Nebraska	NE		
Nevada	NV		
New Hampshire	NH		
New Jersey	NJ		
New Mexico	NM		
New York	NY		
North Carolina	NC		
North Dakota	ND		
Northern Mariana Islands	MP		
Ohio	OH		
Oklahoma	OK		
Oregon	OR		

Use the applications and forms in this section for role plays and more writing practice. Use your own words and ideas.

Unit 1   Extra authentic practice

To _____

Date _____ Time _____   A.M. ☐
                                             P.M. ☐

WHILE YOU WERE OUT

M _____

Phone _____
        Area code   Number   Extension

☐ telephoned   ☐ please call
☐ returned your call   ☐ will call back

Message _____

_____

_____

_____

_____

Unit 2 Extra authentic practice

Brookside Realty
SALES COMMISSION & FEE AGREEMENT

Name: _____

Name: _____

Address: _____

Phone: (H) (_____) _____-_____ (W) (_____) _____-_____

Annual Income: _____ Desired Date of Occupancy: _____

Price Range: _____ - _____

Type of Unit: Condo – 1 Br. 2 Br. 3 Br. 1 Fam. 2 Fam. Multi Fam.

We, BROOKSIDE REALTY, agree to introduce you to various dwellings so that you may purchase one. You agree that any dwellings introduced to you by BROOKSIDE REALTY for sale, you will purchase, make offers to purchase, or have negotiations of any kind only through BROOKSIDE REALTY on these dwellings. If you negotiate the purchase through any other broker on a property introduced to you through BROOKSIDE REALTY, and the seller or other broker does not pay BROOKSIDE REALTY'S commission, you may be held liable for said commission. I (We) agree that if BROOKSIDE REALTY is forced to take legal action as a result of a breach of this agreement, and BROOKSIDE REALTY is the prevailing party, I (we) will be responsible for any legal fees incurred by BROOKSIDE REALTY. I (We) have read and agreed to the aforementioned terms and conditions.

THIS IS A LEGAL AND BINDING AGREEMENT. PLEASE READ IT CAREFULLY BEFORE SIGNING. PLEASE REQUEST A COPY.

Signature: _____ Date: _____

Signature: _____ Date: _____

Unit 3 Extra authentic practice

BENNINGTON AUTO REPAIR
License #770-8162
380 S. Riverside Avenue
Bennington, MI 48164
(616) 555-4528

SERVICE

7242

NAME		CUSTOMER ORDER NO.	DATE
ADDRESS		ORDER WRITTEN BY	PROMISED A.M. / P.M.
CITY, STATE, ZIP			
HOME PHONE	BUS. PHONE	EXT.	ODOMETER
YEAR, MAKE AND MODEL			LICENSE NUMBER
SERIAL NUMBER	MOTOR NUMBER	TERMS	

DESCRIPTION OF WORK

☐ LUBE ☐ CHANGE OIL ☐ OIL FILTER ☐ TUNE-UP ☐ TRANS. ☐ DIFF:

_____ LITERS/GALS. OF GAS @
_____ LITERS/QTS. OF OIL @
_____ kg/LBS. OF GREASE @

	AMOUNT
TOTAL LABOR	
TOTAL PARTS	
ACCESSORIES	
GAS, OIL AND GREASE	
SUBLET REPAIRS	
EPA/WASTE DISPOSAL	
TAX	
TOTAL	

I hereby authorize the above repair work to be done along with the necessary materials. You and your employees may operate above vehicle for purposes of testing, inspection, or delivery at my risk. An express mechanics lien is acknowledged on above vechicle to secure the amount of repairs thereto. It is also understood that you will not be held responsible for loss or damage to cars or articles left in cars in case of fire, theft or any other cause beyond your control.

SIGNATURE

QTY.	PART NO. AND DESCRIPTION	PRICE
	TOTAL PARTS	

ACCESSORIES

	TOTAL ACCESSORIES	

141

Unit 4 Extra authentic practice

HARPER'S
Rain Check

Customer Information:
Last Name: _____ First: _____
Phone Number: _____ Date: _____ Associate Initials: _____

☑ Store Rain check ☐ Request Total # of Cards: _____

Item(s):

SKU/Description	Qty.	Reg. Price	Sale Price
_____	_____	_____	_____
_____	_____	_____	_____
_____	_____	_____	_____
_____	_____	_____	_____

Pick-Up: Customer Signature: _____ Date: _____

Contact Information:
Date: _____ Comments: _____
Date: _____ Comments: _____

SKU# 9018572   Customer copy   Rev 5/00

RAIN CHECKS
Rain checks are not a guarantee of future availability. A rain check assures you the sale price if / when the item becomes available.

Unit 5 Extra authentic practice

MAIL & GO APPLICATION Metro-South Railroad

OFFICIAL USE ONLY

Personal Data (Must Complete)

PLEASE PRINT   Mr./Mrs./Ms. (circle one)   Sex: ❏ Male   ❏ Female

Last Name: _____   First Name: _____   MI: ___

Mailing Address: _____

City: _____   State: _____   Zip: _____ - _____

Home Telephone: _____   Business Telephone: _____
AREA CODE   AREA CODE

Employer Name: _____

Employer Address: _____   City: _____   State: _____   Zip: _____

Travel Information (Must Complete)

Original Station: _____   Destination Station: _____

UniPass Station: _____   Bus Provider/Route #: _____

Receive no value on CityCard, or choose:

- ❏ **$54 Mail & Go *Plus* (*Unlimited* monthly travel; 9% rail fare discount applies)** Value expires at end of month; value cannot be transferred to another CityCard.
- ❏ **$50 Mail & Go *Plus* (44 rides; 9% rail fare discount applies)** Value expires at end of month; value cannot be transferred to another CityCard.
- ❏ **$20 (22 rides; no rail fare discount)** Card good for one year and value can be transferred to another CityCard at any subway station.

Payment Options (Choose One of Three Options Below)

❶ CREDIT CARD OPTION

Please charge the following credit card automatically on the third of each month:

❏ MasterCard ❏ VISA ❏ American Express ❏ Discover

Credit Card Number: _____

Expiration Date: _____ - _____

Print Name of Authorized Cardholder: (as it appears on Credit Card)

_____

Credit Card Billing Address (if different from above mailing address)

_____

I hereby apply for a monthly Mail & Go Ticket and for automatic payment to be made with the above-noted credit card. By signing below I agree to the terms and conditions printed to the left and reverse side of this form for this payment option.

Signature of Authorized Card Holder   Date

❷ PRE-AUTHORIZED DEBIT OPTION

Please debit the following checking account automatically on the third of each month:

Bank Name: _____

Checking Account Number: _____

Offical Use: _____

Name on account: (Both names if joint account. Please print)

_____

Please enclose voided check from Checking Account in pouch provided **here** ⟶

I hereby apply for a monthly Mail & Go Ticket and for automatic payment to be debited from the above-noted checking account. By signing below I agree to the terms and conditions printed to the left and reverse side of this form for this payment option.

Signature   Date

Signature (joint account)   Date

PLACE CHECK HERE

❸ PAYMENT BY CHECK OPTION: ❏ Check Here

I hereby apply for a monthly Mail & Go Ticket. (I agree to pay for my ticket so that payment is received by Metro-South Commuter Railroad by the third day of the month for which the ticket is valid. I will not deduct credits from the invoice amount, and agree to the conditions of use printed to the left and reverse side of this form.)

Signature   Date

TEAR AT PERFORATION AND MOISTEN SEAL

Unit 6 Extra authentic practice

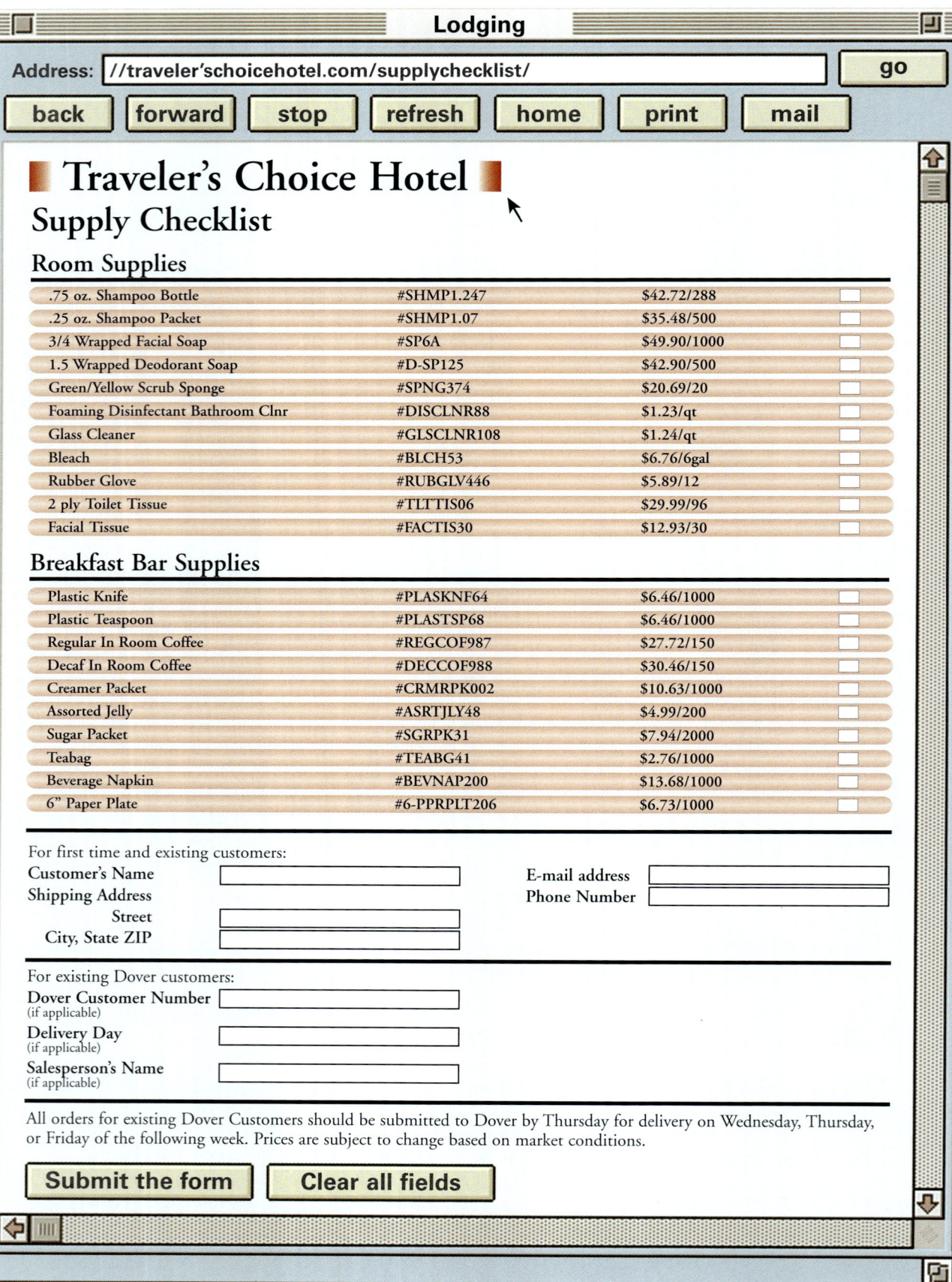

Unit 7 Extra authentic practice

U.S. HealthFirst
HEALTH CLAIM TRANSMITTAL

Employee Name: _____ SSN: ____ - ____ - ____ Date of Birth: ____ / ____ / ____

Employee Address: _____ Check if New Address ❑

Employee Phone Number: (____) _____ Status: ❑ Active ❑ Retired ❑ Continued (COBRA)
                                 Area Code   Number

Spouse Name: _____ Spouse Date of Birth: ____ / ____ / ____

Patient Name: _____ Patient Date of Birth: ____ / ____ / ____ Relationship: _____

Nature of Illness or Injury: _____

_____
IF CLAIM IS DUE TO INJURY STATE WHEN, WHERE AND HOW INJURY OCCURRED

Do You Have More Than One Employer?   Yes ❑   No ❑

Is Your Spouse Employed?   Yes ❑   No ❑

Is Patient Employed?   Yes ❑   No ❑
If you answered "yes" to any of the above questions, please provide the following information:

Employed Person: _____ Social Security Number: ____ - ____ - ____

Employer: _____

Employer Address: _____ Phone Number: (____) _____
                                                                                Area Code   Number

Insurance Company & Policy Number: _____

ANY PERSON WHO KNOWINGLY FILES A STATEMENT OF CLAIM CONTAINING ANY MISREPRESENTATION OR ANY FALSE, INCOMPLETE OR MISLEADING INFORMATION MAY BE GUILTY OF A CRIMINAL ACT PUNISHABLE UNDER LAW AND MAY BE SUBJECT TO CIVIL PENALTIES.

Employee Signature: _____ Date: ____ / ____ / ____

HINTS FOR SUBMITTING CLAIMS TO U.S. HEALTHFIRST

- If you want U.S. HealthFirst to pay benefits directly to the provider of medical services,

  Please sign here _____
- Attach your bills to this completed form and mail to U.S. HealthFirst.
- Make sure all bills indicate the reason (diagnosis) for treatment and list the date, type and cost of each service.
- Send additional bills periodically or when they total $50.00 or more.

For U.S. HealthFirst USE ONLY

DATE BENEFITS BECAME EFFECTIVE						DATE BENEFITS TERMINATED						SUFFIX	ACCOUNT
MO	DAY	YR	MO	DAY	YR	MO	DAY	YR	MO	DAY	YR		
Emp.			Dep.			Emp.			Dep.				

SIGNATURE OF U.S. HEALTHFIRST EMPLOYEE CERTIFYING BENEFITS:	DATE	MO	DAY	YR

Unit 8 Extra authentic practice

NORTH PARK CHILDCARE CENTER
APPLICATION FOR EMPLOYMENT

POSITION DESIRED _____ DATE _____

HOW DID YOU LEARN OF OUR ORGANIZATION? _____

HOURS YOU ARE AVAILABLE TO WORK: Mon   Tues   Wed   Thur   Fri   Sat   Sun

From: _____

☐ Full-Time   ☐ Part-Time   ☐ On-Call   To: _____

I.

NAME _____ SS NUMBER _____
     Last   First   Middle

ADDRESS _____
     Street   City   State   Zip Code

TELEPHONE NO. _____ If necessary, best time to call you at home _____

HAVE YOU EVER FILED AN APPLICATION WITH OR BEEN EMPLOYED BY A DIVISION OF NPCC BEFORE? _____ If yes, give date(s) _____

ARE YOU CERTIFIED TO PERFORM INFANT OR TODDLER CPR? _____

ARE YOU LEGALLY ELIGIBLE FOR EMPLOYMENT IN THE UNITED STATES? _____
(Proof of U.S. Citizenship or immigration status will be required upon employment)

HAVE YOU EVER BEEN CONVICTED OF A MISDEMEANOR OR A FELONY IN ANY JURISDICTION?
_____ If yes, describe in detail: _____
_____

II. Employment Experience

A. EMPLOYER _____ Address _____

Dates of Employment _____ Salary _____

Telephone No. _____ Supervisor _____

Describe your work _____

Why did you leave? _____

May we contact this employer? _____ Yes _____ No

Unit 9 Extra authentic practice

Please complete the entire application in blue or black ink to ensure the fastest response.

Please show us how you would like your name to appear on the Card.
Please spell the last name completely. (Full name must not exceed 20 spaces.)

Personal Information

(Optional) ☐ Mr. ☐ Mrs. ☐ Miss ☐ Ms. ☐ Dr.

		Mo.	Day	Yr.
First, Middle, Last Name (Please print above)		Date of Birth		
Home Address (Apt. #, if any)	City	State		Zip
Yrs. Mos.	( )	— —		
Time at Current Address Home Phone	Social Security Number	E-Mail Address (optional)		
$	$			
Annual Personal Gross Income	Additional Personal Income*	Source of Additional Income†		

☐ Own Home   *Minimum Personal Yearly Income—$15,000
☐ Rent   †Include salary, income from savings and source (banker, broker, employer, etc.) whom we can call for confirmation
(alimony, separate maintenance, or child support need not be revealed if you do not wish to rely on it.)

Business and Financial Information

		( )
Employer or Firm Name		Business Phone
Business Street Address	City	State Zip
	Yrs. Mos. ☐ Full-Time Student ☐ Self-Employed ☐ Retired	
Position at Firm	Time There	

Do you have any of the following?
Checking Account ☐ Yes ☐ No   Savings Account (includes Money Market, CD) ☐ Yes ☐ No
☐ Major/Other Credit Card   ☐ Department Store/Retail   ☐ Gas/Oil
Bank Name

Please sign below.
Additional information may be requested by us for further processing when you apply with this form. By signing below, I certify that I have read, met, and agreed to all of the terms, conditions, and disclosures on this application.

X _____
Signature of Applicant (Please do not print.)   Date

Please fill in the following to obtain an Additional Card.
For $30 a year you can obtain an Additional Card for qualified individuals age 18 or older.

First, Middle, Last Name (Please print.)
Month Day Year   — —
Date of Birth   Social Security Number

147

Unit 10 Extra authentic practice

HMO Enrollment/Change Application

| HMO Name | HMO Plan State | HMO Group/Policy Number | Division | Coverage Effective Date |

Employee Last Name ____ First Name ____ MI ____ Hire Date ____ Birth Date ____ Sex ☐ Male ☐ Female Social Security Number ____

HMO Coverage Category: ☐ Employee Only ☐ Employee +1 ☐ Employee + Family

Street Address *(Must Live in HMO Service Area)* ____ City ____ State ____ Zip ____ Country ____

Employee Status: ☐ Active ☐ COBRA ☐ Retiree

Type of Enrollment: ☐ Open Enrollment ☐ New Hire

☐ Change: ___ Life Status Change ___ Relocation/Transfer ___ Other

Marital Status: ☐ Single ☐ Married ☐ Separated ☐ Divorced

Location ____ Home Phone ( ) ____ Work Phone ( ) ____

Eligible Dependents

Full Name *(First, MI, Last)*	Birth Date *(mm/dd/yy)*	Sex *(M/F)*	Relationship	Social Security Number	College Name and Location *(For Full-time College Students)*	Choice of Primary Care Physician or Health Center	Physician/Center Code
	/ /		self				
	/ /		spouse				
	/ /						
	/ /						
	/ /						

Dentist *(if applicable)* ____ Code ____ Pharmacy *(if applicable)* ____ Code ____

Information About Other Medical Coverage

Do you, your spouse, or any enrolled dependents have Medicare coverage? ☐ Yes ☐ No

If yes, show for whom ☐ Self ☐ Spouse ☐ Dependent name ____

Medicare No./Health Ins. No. *(Claim No.)* ____

Effective Dates: Part A / /   Part B / /

Do your spouse or dependents have other group hospital medical insurance? ☐ Yes ☐ No

Covered Member Name(s) ____
Employer Name ____
Employer Address ____
Employer Phone ____
Insurance Company Name ____
Policy Group Member ____

ENROLLMENT AGREEMENT AND PAYROLL DEDUCTION AUTHORIZATION

I certify that I have reviewed all of the statements in this application and that they are true and complete. I apply for coverage with the HMO indicated above for the person(s) listed on this form. I agree that I and all my eligible dependents shall abide by the provisions of coverage in the service agreement of the HMO under which we are enrolled. The subscriber contract which I am issued will determine the rights and responsibilities of member(s) and will govern in the event of conflicts with any benefits comparison or summary description of the HMO Plan.

On behalf of myself and my eligible dependents, I hereby authorize all hospitals, physicians, and medical service providers and other organizations (including insurers and any prepaid health plan) to give the HMO (or its representative) access to relevant medical, prescription drug, employment, and insurance coverage records. I understand that both on my behalf, and on behalf of my eligible dependents, as a condition for the receipt of benefits and services, the above mentioned entities have the right to share and review these records.

This information will be utilized by the HMO to verify services performed for me and my eligible dependents, and also for utilization review and quality assurance, this authorization shall remain valid for the term of this coverage.

EMPLOYEE SIGNATURE: ____ DATE: ____